THE PLAYBOOK

SIX PLAYS AND ONE LIBRETTO

EPHINY GALE

This first edition published by Foxgrove Press, Melbourne, Victoria, Australia, in December 2016

CAUTION: All rights to the plays within (including those of professional or amateur performance, video or sound recordings, adaptation, translation, or reproduction of any kind) are reserved. These scripts are subject to royalties. Please consult www.ephinygale.com for information regarding obtaining rights and any related enquiries.

IBSN: 9780995435308

For Tara,
whom I met through the magic of theatre

CONTENTS

Introduction 9

Time Scraps 17
A drama in three acts

Back from Fairy Land 51
A drama in three acts

Tether 67
A drama in one act

How to Direct from Inside 103
A drama in one act

Match Girls 147
A drama in one act

Sir Santino and the Excessive Cut-to 177
A comedy in three acts

Shining Armour 217
A musical drama in two acts

About Ephiny Gale 271

INTRODUCTION

When asked whether I've seen a particular movie (or read a particular book), I reply fairly often with, "No, but I've read the script."

I enjoy reading scripts just as much as prose, and often more than seeing a fully produced play or film. When I'm reading a script I can direct it however I like, in the fully-flexible theatre inside my head.

I do wish that there were more recent stage scripts published in collections like this one. For my own reading pleasure, and for theatre companies, and perhaps for school students who would prefer to read about their contemporaries than study yet another Shakespeare play. These pages are my own small contribution to the world of published stage plays: several of the works I'm most proud of from the last eight years.

The very first play I remember writing was a five minute skit in French for Year 8 French class. The second (although I'm sure there were some in between) was a monologue for Year 11 English. My generous English teacher went out of her way to stop me in the courtyard and let me know how much she liked it. This is my clearest memory of high school.

Regardless, without my time in student theatre at university, none of these scripts would probably have existed. I am very grateful for those years, which allowed me to write, direct and act in so many plays. For anyone who wishes to be a playwright, or in fact a writer of any kind, my advice is this: involve yourself in as much theatre as possible, in as many different roles as possible. And watch all of your movies and TV with subtitles.

#

ON THE PLAYS WITHIN

The following introductory notes include mild spoilers and may be read before or after the plays at your leisure.

Time Scraps

While no longer an especially recent work, this is probably still the play I'm most proud of. I remember how excited I was when *Time Scraps* was shortlisted for St Martin's National Playwriting Competition, the first place I'd submitted it to, recently-finished.

This play sprang to life, primarily, as a result of the following: discussions of time travel whilst eating chocolate dumplings at a birthday party; my good friend Clara Pagone suggesting I write something with a small cast, piles of books, and a balloon (I may have ignored that last one); and reading about the mouse in *Flowers for Algernon*.

I'm especially pleased with the piecemeal nature of the scenes in *Time Scraps*. Partially because they create the sort of disjointed sense of time that I think benefits the story, and partially because I love a non-linear narrative, but also because the visuals and scenarios on stage are constantly moving. My favourite kind of stories are often fast-paced and ambiguous, the kind that only make complete sense at the end, once you've collated all the scraps.

Aside from time travel, this is a play about shame. And to those who've asked me why it includes lesbians, in an aren't-the-lesbians-sort-of-gratuitous kind of way, I say, "Really? *Really?* Look again."

Back from Fairy Land

I often start work on plays based on a staging concept. Prior to writing this one, I'd been watching several Open2Study MOOCs where the tutors draw on glass walls between themselves and the camera. I'd never seen that (or anything similar) incorporated into a play before, and I particularly enjoy placing my characters under physical restrictions, so I morphed the single glass wall into a glass cube.

It was a lot of fun to write a portal fantasy aimed at adults with a younger teenager as the protagonist, which is not a combination one usually encounters. I appreciate portal fantasies more and more as I get older: there are few situations more inherently wondrous and delightful.

When I was 14 I spent two months on school camp in the middle of the bush, which I enjoyed far less than Madalyn enjoys visiting Minellothi. It was, however, an interesting exercise in feeling displaced from my normal life in the city. Two months is a very long time when you're 14. Primarily, I learnt how little any adult seemed to care about my experiences away from home, whether it was before the camp, during the camp or afterwards.

I think you can pick the more recent plays in this collection (in terms of writing date) by those which discuss one's responsibility, particularly in regards to other people. As I continue to age and gain responsibilities, so do my characters. *Back from Fairy Land* is the last script I wrote in this collection.

Tether

How to Direct From Inside enjoyed a sold-out season at La Mama in 2009, and although I was thoroughly pleased with both the script and the production, I was also aware that about a third of the audience left the theatre feeling rather confused. Following this, *Tether* was my attempt to write something more mainstream and easily digestible.

Nine characters in *Tether* (excluding John, who is the tenth) are loosely based on the nine types of the Enneagram personality typing system. The Enneagram focuses on everyone's different key needs (e.g. 'ones' need to be perfect, 'twos' need to feel needed, 'threes' need success...) so it was a useful framework for starting to discuss the characters' sense of meaning and belonging in the world.

Tether is my most realistic script, and it makes me slightly uncomfortable in the same way that real life often does: with its awkwardness and uncertainly and, as John says, the brushing the teeth parts.

How to Direct from Inside

I owe much of the success of this script to Clara Pagone. She was the first to step into the role of Blue, back in 2008 when we won the Best Five Minute Play award at Dante's with what later became scene one of *How to Direct from Inside*. Soon after that she directed a flawless first production of the full-length play. I am grateful for her talent, professionalism, and ongoing friendship.

The essence of this story is simple: a young woman has various personas, which are then thrown into turmoil. Because the genre is magic realism, the way this presents to the audience is more complicated than it otherwise might be, but the storyline itself is not complex. How we present ourselves to others—the different facets and faces we show to different people—has been an ongoing fascination of mine for most of my life. Eventually, I hope to end up more like Eve at the end of this play, but in the meantime I still have work to do.

To clarify a couple of small misconceptions that have frustrated me in the past: Red and Blue were never together. And 'domestic' Blue doesn't mean 'romantic' Blue: it means Blue at home, which is (for her) usually completely unromantic.

Every day, I pass a photo of the original cast on my bookcase. I am reminded of everyone's warmth and skill, and the wonderful aesthetic of that first show, with candles and matches and dolls and silk. My sincere thanks to everyone who helped make that production a reality.

Match Girls

This play was developed specifically for The Container Festival, which meant that it would be performed in a shipping container with a stage width of about 2.5 metres. Sitting in such a small, dimly lit space with about 14 other audience members seemed to naturally lend itself to storytelling. The relative darkness emphasises the words. I do miss the kind of storytelling that is shared by a group in the dark, which doesn't seem to happen any more once you grow out of childhood. Add a few glimpses of faces and hands in the match light and the experience is complete.

I originally wrote the three tales in this play as three separate short stories. For *Match Girls* they've been heavily edited to form a coherent whole. By 'whole,' I don't mean that they necessarily intersect from a plot point of view, though they could arguably occur within the same universe. I do mean that they intersect together to form a larger storytelling experience, a rhythm, that they weave together like a DJ may blend songs in and out of each other. They provide contrast and shade to one another, and offer thematic through-lines in the same way that the plays in this wider collection repeat themes and character types and plot elements.

As the title suggests, this is a play about burning. The main characters burn others, burn themselves, or are burnt *by* others. Burning is a common way to die in fairy tales, particularly for villains. And of course, history is written by the victors.

I am not at all afraid of fire, but I am a little afraid of being burnt to death, in the same way that I'm afraid of a pitchfork-thrusting mob chasing me down the street. As it is in *Match Girls*, it's easy for people to despise you when your intentions are misunderstood, or when your humanity is forgotten.

I end this play on a hopeful note because I am hopeful. That there is love and light amongst the darkness. That stories are shared, that empathy grows, that lanterns are lit. That a more compassionate world can grow out of the ashes.

Sir Santino and the Excessive Cut-to

My works are certainly not exclusively dark, and *Sir Santino* is probably the silliest play I've ever written. A lot of it is also aggressively random. At the time of writing *Sir Santino* I was feeling particularly stifled at work, and was grateful for the opportunity to write something a bit *excessive*.

This is a script about excess, and in particular an excess of feelings. Our (anti)hero Santino has the emotional control of a small child, and his feelings tend to burst forth and literally interrupt and displace the lives of others. I had been writing a couple of screenplays in the months before starting *Sir Santino* and wanted to incorporate filmic techniques in a stage play in a way I'd never seen done before. Thus, the cut-tos were born.

When I re-visited *Sir Santino* for this collection I was initially worried that some elements seemed somewhat anti-feminist, particularly in contrast to some of my other plays. However, I hope that any of Santino's problematic behaviour is painted in a suitably negative light. Helena is always the one in charge in their relationship, and her frequent cooking and cleaning is much more about her status as an independent adult (in contrast to Santino) than it is about performing a traditional female role. She's certainly not performing any duties for Santino's sake. Lastly, it seems somewhat strange to me that Helena would fall for Santino at all, but I'm often bewildered that women are interested in most men.

Reading this script can still make me laugh out loud, several years later. I should say that some of the jokes are intentionally not funny, and are thus amusing to me *because* of their not-funny-ness. Obviously, your own experience may vary.

Shining Armour

I did question the inclusion of a libretto in this collection, simply because librettos often read very strangely as scripts without their accompanying music. Much of the tone of the piece, its rhythm, and its emotion is lost. But this is my most popular musical, and I decided it still had a place here in libretto form.

If you're reading this without the music (which is likely), allow me to give you the general feeling: almost all of the songs are sung out of the characters' desperation. This is not a happy musical. There are upbeat moments, there are manic moments, there are moments of determination and bravado, but that is not the same as genuine joy or contentment. Don't be fooled.

Also, this is (at first glance) a piece about fairy tales. But really, it's set in a world with no magic at all. The visual landscape I imagine for the show is quite drab: muted earth tones with occasional bursts of brighter fake magic. If you're familiar with musicals, think the *Spring Awakening* set; not *Wicked*, not Disney.

Shining Armour is a deconstruction, not a parody. If in doubt, pull back. Yes, there are humorous moments, but if it gets too funny, or too cartoonish, its message is lost.

This is a musical about the power of stories. Obviously I adore stories in general, but when false stories (such as fairy tales) are considered the unquestionable truth, then you have a big problem.

Seeing this show on stage at The 1812 Theatre for the first time was absolutely electrifying, and I'm thoroughly grateful to everyone who contributed, particularly Zaverr Doctor, Tayla Thomas and Maria Roitman, who played the three central characters with fantastic aplomb. My favourite songs in *Shining Armour* are "That kind of witch", "Damn hard", "Eighteen", and "Give me the road", but I wish I could play them all for you right now.

FINALLY, IN CONCLUSION

To everyone who has ever been involved in my theatre making, whether as cast, crew, audience, or simply by reading my scripts: thank you for joining me on these adventures. Here's to a world full of theatre, scripts, books, stories and strangeness.

- Ephiny Gale, 2016

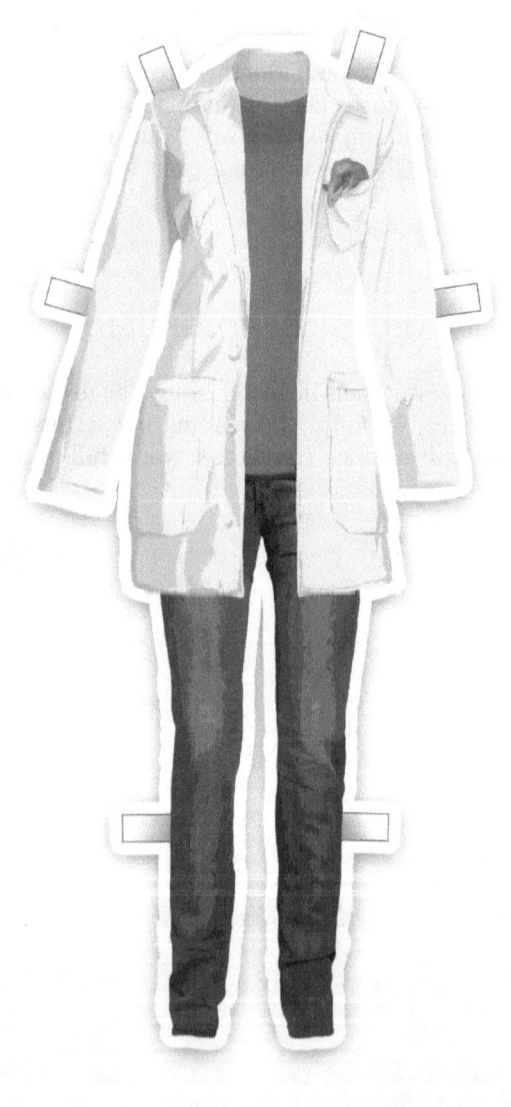

TIME SCRAPS

CHARACTERS (in order of appearance):

JILL: Scientist. Perfectionist.
JACK: Scientist. Superhero enthusiast. Frightened of the future.
SADIE SMITH: Children's dance teacher. Gentle and wide-eyed. Significant memory issues.

SETTING:

Melbourne, Australia. 2007.

A NOTE ON FORMATTING:

A forward slash (/) is used to indicate when the next character begins speaking before the first character has finished their line(s). Wherever a forward slash appears inside a character's dialogue, the next character should begin to say their line(s) immediately. This will lead to two characters speaking at the same time for at least a moment; this is wholly intentional and is mandatory for all productions.

ACT ONE

- **SCENE ONE**

Entirely off-stage:

JILL: Did you take Alabama out of her cage?

JACK: She's not in there?

JILL: You see that bloody pile in the corner?

JACK: I hope you're joking.

JILL: What if it worked?

JACK: The time machine wouldn't... do that. She'll turn up. *(beat)* Go on, Jill, I'll clean this.

JILL: Wait. *(elated)* What if it worked?

- **SCENE TWO (BOOK FIVE)**

SADIE SMITH (23) addresses an unseen camera.

Three large, open notebooks (Books One, Three and Five) sit nearby, all of distinctly different colours and design. Each subsequent scene comes from one of these notebooks, which should be made apparent by whichever notebook is highlighted during that scene.

Currently we are in Book Five.

JILL: *(offstage)* March 5, 2007.

SADIE: My name is Sadie Smith. My brother froze to death when I was 12. I don't remember the cold, although it must have been. I just remember his breathing. And on any given day, if it's more than 48 hours ago, I probably don't remember much before that, either.

- **SCENE THREE (BOOK THREE)**

A section of an old factory refurbished into a lab. This is home for those who work here: the walls are covered with bookshelves, blueprints and diagrams, a hand-made metal butterfly, an old superman postcard...

JILL (28) hands SADIE a takeaway coffee, keeping one for herself. She switches on her laptop. Waits for it to start up.

JILL: So what do you do, Sadie?

SADIE: Oh, I'm... a dance teacher. For little kids.

JILL: Really? How long have you been doing that?

SADIE: Couple of years. Do you dance?

JILL: No! Oh, badly. Funny, I never would've picked you. Do you enjoy it?

SADIE: Yes. Very much.

JILL: I try to go running sometimes.

SADIE: Do you work here full-time?

JILL: The grant doesn't stretch that far. I'm here three days a week, three days at a car company.

SADIE: Car company?

JILL: Here's much more interesting.

- **SCENE FOUR (BOOK ONE)**

Black.

JACK: Ms Smith, we'd really appreciate it if you did the occasional video recording as well as the journals.

SADIE: But... what for?

JACK: It's a different way to present you, should our research get published. It's more personal.

SADIE: But what do I say?

The lights slowly rise. SADIE looks shell-shocked by the camera JACK (29) is operating.

JACK: Just... about you and your involvement. You've been through the interview. You know what we're interested in.

JILL: March 5, 2007.

Silence.

SADIE: I'd rather not.

JILL: Why not?

SADIE: It feels like a performance. You won't really get anything.

JILL: Shut the camera, Jack.

SADIE: I'm sorry.

JILL: It's alright.

SADIE: You went to so much trouble... Randomly selecting a journal and all. Can that just be enough?

- **SCENE FIVE (BOOK FIVE)**

SADIE and JILL talking on their respective phones:

SADIE: They were going to execute me. String me up by my wrists 'til my mind fuzzed out and hunger took me. But I didn't want to die like that; I took a gun. Flicked off the safety catch. Pressed it to my gut and imagined the bullet ripping through and the world contracting. Like pupils. 'Til there's no light left and it's just nothing. Empty. Stopped. And then it felt like my gut really had been ripped out, because how could I leave this behind?

JILL: It's only a dream.

SADIE: I put down the gun and went out with a fight.

- **SCENE SIX (BOOK THREE)**

JACK holds a long tray of six cups in front of SADIE.

SADIE: How is this different from the doors? Or the boxes?

JACK: It's not; it's exactly the same.

SADIE: And what is this telling you?

JACK: If I told you, it would ruin the experiment.

SADIE: And I just choose a cup?

JACK: You just choose a cup.

SADIE: But there seems to be a right answer. And I don't understand how that can be, from random guessing.

JACK: Why do you think that?

SADIE: Because when I chose the door, you started to smile. And when I chose the box, you started to grin.

JACK: Well, I apologise. I didn't mean to.

Silence. SADIE points to the cup second-from-the-right.

SADIE: I choose that one.

JACK starts to grin again. Quickly wipes it from his face.

SADIE: Well, I guess I'm wrong. I couldn't guess right that many times.

JACK: Don't assume anything.

- **SCENE SEVEN (BOOK FIVE)**

An envelope falls from the ceiling. No one notices. No one touches it.

- **SCENE EIGHT (BOOK ONE)**

JACK and JILL sit on one side of the table, SADIE on the other.

JACK: So when you say you have a terrible memory, what do you mean?

SADIE: I mean... if it happened more than a week ago, it may as well never have happened at all.

JILL: And it's not a clinical problem?

SADIE: I don't think so. I haven't seen anyone about it, but no one's ever said anything.

JACK: They haven't said anything?

SADIE: No. I mean... I have ways to get around it.

JILL: So what can't you remember? I mean, you remember your friends, you remember the way to work after a holiday?

SADIE: It depends on the friend. Usually I just know if I like someone or not, in my gut, but I don't know why. And directions are hard, if I can't just be on autopilot. I get lost a lot.

JACK: So you remember the result of an interaction on an emotional level, but not what brought you there in the first place.

SADIE: Yes.

JACK and JILL glance at each other. They rise.

JACK: If you'll bear with us a moment, Sadie, we'd like to take you through some choices. We'd like you to pick one of the following doors...

- **SCENE NINE (BOOK FIVE)**

SADIE and JILL over dinner:

JILL: Did you always want to be a dance teacher?

SADIE: Oh... No, I wanted to do lots of different things. What about you?

JILL: I don't know... I think I wanted to be a zoologist for a while, but the parents didn't like that. That might be why I ended up here. They don't see the benefit right now, but I was working on the ultimate way to make them happy. To never go wrong again.

SADIE: No, never. Pity it doesn't work like that.

JILL: Mmmm.

SADIE: And how's everything besides work?

JILL: Oh, getting a bit of running in some mornings. The garden's looking great, planted some gorgeous flowers on the weekend. But you know, the work's what I'm passionate about. That's where my energy goes.

SADIE: I'd love to see your flowers sometime.

Silence.

JILL: Yeah. You should. *(beat)* You're a really good listener, you know.

SADIE: I have to be if I've forgotten everything about you. *(beat)* You didn't notice? I haven't asked you anything specific all evening.

JILL: Well...

SADIE: Anything you hadn't already brought up tonight.

JILL: Oh.

SADIE: I've had practice.

JILL: So we'll never run out of conversation.

▪ SCENE TEN (BOOK ONE)

SADIE's flat. She selects a notebook from one of the large piles. She flicks through it pensively until she spots something:

SADIE: *(reading)* November 14, 2002.

I met Esther's friend Jill tonight. She's got to be one of the prettiest girls I've ever seen. She's really nice, too. I talked to her a little at the party, but mostly hung around with Esther trying not to make a fool of myself. Esther doesn't know if she likes girls, but apparently Jill's parents won't let her date anyone anyway. But no one's ever allowed to date me. We can be secret agents. I'm really sneaky when I want to be. She smells like jellybeans and spice and old roses.

SADIE starts to choke and runs to the garbage bin to dry retch. She throws the notebook at the wall, then takes a moment to recover before replacing it in the pile.

- **SCENE ELEVEN (BOOK THREE)**

A cold, dark room. A shaft of light shines through the doorway. JACK and JILL stand unseen on the other side.

SADIE: How long am I in here?

JACK: Two hours.

SADIE crouches. She puts her hands on the floor but retracts them immediately.

SADIE: The floor is freezing!

JACK: It's not supposed to be comfortable, Sadie.

SADIE: I thought I chose the doors right.

JILL: Yes, but you weren't sure enough.

SADIE mouths something in the silence.

JACK: We'll collect you when it's time.

One pair of footsteps retreat. A thin torchlight rolls under the door, and then the other pair leave. SADIE flicks the torch on.

- **SCENE TWELVE (BOOK FIVE)**

JACK opens a small cage and hands SADIE a mouse.

JACK: Sadie, this is Florida.

SADIE: Hello, Florida.

JILL: She's done similar tests to yours.

SADIE: *(to Florida)* And did you do as well as me?

JILL: Both your results were statistically significant.

SADIE: Why'd you need me, then? If you could get results from a mouse?

JILL: Florida's quite a pioneer. She's the first mouse to show any effect from time travel.

SADIE: Bad memory?

JACK: No, mice act on their instincts well enough. We found half of Alabama to Arizona in a bloody mess in their cages, and then two days later their other halves in the silver box. After that we re-evaluated the time machine.

JILL: We don't put anyone inside any more.

- **SCENE THIRTEEN (BOOK ONE)**

JACK stands in front of an unseen camera.

JACK: It's not that difficult, Ms Smith. May I call you Sadie? I'll give a demonstration.

(to the camera) My name is Jack Milton. I've been working here for about three years now, and I believe we've developed the first unfalsifiable time machine. Ever since I was a kid in a superman costume, I always wanted to fly fast enough to change the rotation of the earth. I figured changing time would be easier than flying. This morning I ate French toast. I really hate stuffed bunny rabbits.

(to Sadie) Now you.

- **SCENE FOURTEEN (BOOK THREE)**

SADIE and JILL on their respective phones:

SADIE: Hi, it's Sadie.

JILL: Sadie! Not to be rude, but how did you get my number?

SADIE: Jack gave it to me. I'm sorry, should I not be calling?

JILL: No, it's fine. I'm in the lab anyway. Is something wrong?

SADIE: I was just thinking... What happened to all the mice between Arizona and Florida?

JILL: Nothing happened to them. We figured, chances are, we've probably already wound back time at least once. We would have conditioned a few mice before then. We tested all of them, and Florida was the first one to show results.

SADIE: Did you send Florida back again?

JILL: No, we figured we'd get stuck in a loop. We wanted to try with someone like you. The world might actually listen to that, even with a time machine impossible to prove.

SADIE: But the mice came back in pieces.

JILL: Still, impossible to prove that happened because their time print got torn.

Silence.

JILL: Sadie?

SADIE: Ummm... When was that? When you tested it the first time?

JILL: About 20 months ago now. Why?

SADIE: About then, I woke up one morning and I could dance.

- **SCENE FIFTEEN (BOOK ONE)**

JACK stands in front of SADIE with the tray of cups. She points to the third from the left.

SADIE: That one.

JACK nods at her to drink it. Cautiously, she does. And spits it straight back in: it's completely foul.

JACK: (*instructing*) You want the one second from the right.

SADIE takes the lemonade and gulps it down.

- **SCENE SIXTEEN (BOOK THREE)**

SADIE and JILL sit on the floor with Florida's cage.

JILL: Have you really thought about this? You could do anything.

SADIE: I'm thinking about it.

JILL: You could be the world's best dancer. You've got all the time in the world, you just rewind the earth.

SADIE: Yes.

JILL: You can live forever.

SADIE: Sort of. *(beat)* Jealous?

JILL: I like things to be temporary.

- **SCENE SEVENTEEN (BOOK FIVE)**

SADIE holds a hand-held video camera in front of her face.

SADIE: Roll up, roll up! See the world's first working time machine! Only we can never, ever say for certain whether it works. Tell us, Jack!

JACK looks sceptically at the camera.

JACK: I hope you're not showing this footage to anyone. The time machine is still confidential, even this close to D-Day.

SADIE: Of course not. This is just for our records.

JACK: Well, then, ladies and gentlemen. The time machines in the movies have led you terribly astray. They ask you to believe that when you travel back in time, you split yourself in two and effectively arc over the timeline to a previous point. Not only is it impossible to split yourself, as proved by poor bloodied Arizona, it is impossible to arc over the line. You cannot travel back in time to a location. We now believe that the only effective method of time travel is to rewind time, like you rewind a video tape, back to the point you've specified. The time machine is not a transportation device but a metaphorical VCR.

SADIE zooms in on a small metal box. This is the time machine. It is unimpressive besides a few buttons, a basic display screen and some wiring visible behind glass.

SADIE: And as we've rewound everything, including our records and memories, no one can remember pushing the rewind button in the first place. So it can't ever be proven. The average Joe would think it completely useless. Presumably, you are going to repeat the same actions over and over again because you've arrived at the same set of circumstances as the first time.

SADIE shoves the camera up in JILL's face.

SADIE: But of course, ladies and gents, soon-to-be world-famous scientist Jill French is much too brilliant for that.

JILL: We figured that like a video tape, the rewind process might have some after-effects. Like if you rewind a tape too much and it starts to wear. That maybe, if you weren't used to remembering how you learnt something in the first place, the information you learnt before the rewind might actually stick. You're a little bit different, but you don't remember how or why. Most people are going to rebel against that. Most people are going to go back to how they were before.

SADIE: Why the hell are we keeping these records, anyway?

- **SCENE EIGHTEEN (BOOK ONE)**

SADIE sits on the desk, Florida's cage on her lap. She slides a letter back inside an envelope identical to the one that fell in scene seven.

SADIE: I'm going to time travel, Florida! I'll be unconsciously competent. That's where you make a mistake, so you don't do it that way any more, and you don't do it that way so often until you do it right without even thinking.

You're so pretty, Florida! You're a mouse! *(giggles)* Oh, come on, don't look at me like that. We're a team, you and I. A couple of lab experiments wandering blindly off into the unknown. Things have been a bit sad lately, but who knew I was going to turn out so special? They don't have much evidence for time travel without us. We're really something now.

- **SCENE NINETEEN (BOOK ONE)**

SADIE, JACK and JILL stand around the time machine.

JACK: You ready?

SADIE: Yes.

JILL: You don't have any doubts?

SADIE: No, I'm good. But... it's just us.

JILL: Who should there be?

SADIE: I don't know. A camera crew or something?

JACK: Whatever they recorded would be wiped when you pushed that button.

SADIE: Oh. Of course.

JILL: *(hugging her)* Good luck next time.

JACK:			Remember your doors and boxes.

SADIE laughs. She raises her hand... and presses the button. Snap to black.

END OF ACT ONE

ACT TWO

- **SCENE TWENTY (BOOK THREE)**

Book One should now be permanently closed.

SADIE perches on Jill's desk, eating takeaway from a plastic container. JILL is engrossed in her laptop computer.

SADIE: Have you thought about going back further?

JILL: How much further?

SADIE: Say, 15 years?

JILL: Well, it wouldn't do much to help the research. In fact, it would probably hinder it.

Silence.

I don't know if it would do anything at all for you, Sadie. Your brain wouldn't be in the formal operational stage back then. You may not be able to process anything you'd learnt here. *(beat)* Besides, how was your memory back then?

SADIE: *(beat)* A lot better.

- **SCENE TWENTY-ONE (BOOK FIVE)**

SADIE kneels on the floor, Florida's cage between her knees.

SADIE: I think Florida's sick, guys.

JACK: She's old, Sadie. Mice usually live one to two years. Florida's past that already.

SADIE:	But I can't help thinking, maybe the rewinds are doing something to her.
JILL:	Like the wear on the tape?
SADIE:	Yes.
JILL:	Well, it's possible, I suppose.
SADIE:	You said I must have rewound a couple of times at least. Already. What if it's limited? What if I can't do it forever or something terrible will happen?
JACK:	There's nothing to suggest that.
SADIE:	Well, of course there isn't.
JILL:	We can't ever know, Sadie. We just have to keep going in good faith. Florida's already lived to a ripe old age.
SADIE:	Where are you going to bury her?

JACK and JILL just look at each other.

SADIE:	Can I have her?
JILL:	Sure, when she passes on.

SADIE nods.

- **SCENE TWENTY-TWO (BOOK THREE)**

JILL finishes reading the letter. She hands it to SADIE, who slides it carefully back into an envelope identical to the one which fell in scene seven.

SADIE successfully holds back tears. She shrugs. JILL hugs her.

- **SCENE TWENTY-THREE (BOOK FIVE)**

SADIE and JILL run in from the garden.

SADIE: Your flowers... are beautiful.

A surprisingly comfortable moment. JILL kisses her.

JILL: This is a secret.

SADIE: This is a secret.

JILL: This is a secret.

SADIE: This is a secret.

JILL: This is a—

SADIE cuts her off with another kiss.

- **SCENE TWENTY-FOUR (BOOK THREE)**

SADIE and JILL amongst Sadie's piles of journals.

JILL: God! I knew you had to keep them, but I had no idea there'd be so many. I bet you're up here all the time.

SADIE: Not really.

JILL: Not really? But aren't these your replacement memory?

JILL picks one up, and is about to flick through it when SADIE takes it from her.

SADIE: Yeah... Sometimes.

JILL: I don't mean to pry. It's just, this is fascinating... This is your whole life up here.

SADIE: Yes.

JILL: Could we publish some of this?

SADIE: No! God, I have enough trouble keeping these in the first place.

JILL: What do you mean?

SADIE: Well, it's not like I read them, usually.

JILL: I don't understand.

SADIE: They make me ill.

JILL: But they're your thoughts.

SADIE: No, they're not. They *were* my thoughts. They don't count for anything now.

Silence.

JILL: Is this why you haven't had your memory checked out?

SADIE: Well, I started to. I even got a referral. But then I forgot to follow up on it.

JILL: Forgot on purpose.

SADIE: They make me sick, Jill. They make me so sick.

- **SCENE TWENTY-FIVE (BOOK FIVE)**

JACK and JILL lean over the balcony.

JACK: You don't think we're giving Sadie too much freedom?

Silence.

JILL: Maybe a little.

- **SCENE TWENTY-SIX (BOOK THREE)**

SADIE sits at the table.

SADIE: So why are we keeping records?

JILL: Well...

JACK: We tried to send them back through the machine. They turned out even worse than the mice: just useless. But that won't always be the case. One day, we'll develop a method of getting them back intact, and we can send a proper record back in time.

SADIE: But you still don't know... now.

JILL: But we might by the time we send you back.

SADIE: I see.

JILL: You're having doubts?

SADIE: I'm just picturing this whole process going on for a while.

JACK: Well... You see, the grant runs out very soon if we can't prove what we're doing. But the beauty of it is we have forever.

SADIE: But neither of you change.

JACK: We don't think so, no. But you do.

- **SCENE TWENTY-SEVEN (BOOK FIVE)**

SADIE spots the envelope from scene seven on the ground. It hasn't moved since then.

SADIE: Hey, a letter!

She swoops to pick it up, but JILL grabs her from behind before she reaches it. They're both laughing. They kiss easily.

JILL: Do you think we've done this before?

SADIE: I don't know. Do you think we have?

JILL: I don't know. Do you know what to do?

SADIE: Do I know what to do?

JILL: That's not what I meant.

SADIE: You mean do I know what you like?

JILL makes an affirmative noise.

SADIE: *(beat)* Earlobe.

JILL: You stay away from my earlobe!

SADIE: So this is the first time!

JILL: Does that bother you?

SADIE: No, it's interesting.

JILL laughs.

JILL: Read me your journals.

SADIE: No!

JILL: Come on, just a page or two. It can be from last year.

SADIE: No, absolutely not!

JILL approaches a pile of journals.

SADIE: I mean it!

JILL: Fine, then! But I don't know what the problem is.

SADIE: That's fine.

JILL: What is it you want to forget so much?

SADIE: Nothing... Nothing in particular.

JILL: You have lots of regrets.

SADIE: No regrets.

JILL: Of course not.

SADIE: I mean, you do the best you can at the time. That's all you can do.

JILL: Of course.

SADIE: What's your issue?

JILL: I'm just wondering what you think is so bad. Are there conspiracies in here or something?

SADIE: No, of course not.

JILL: Then what's the problem?

SADIE: What...? I... Look, it's just...

JILL starts to read one of them.

SADIE: Fine! Alright. You want to know what's inside? You don't have to read them! I can make it up right now:

Look, here comes Jill, she's the centre of the earth. Let's worship her feet. If I'm with her, I can just die right now—impale me right through the heart. And... her lips are red as volcanoes and the sun shines out her arse. Here comes Jill, she smells like fireflies. Hang me up and let my blood run dry!

JILL leaves.

- **SCENE TWENTY-EIGHT (BOOK THREE)**

SADIE stands in front of the unseen video camera.

JILL: *(offstage)* March 5, 2007.

SADIE: Uh... My name is Sadie. They picked me because I have a terrible memory. I was mostly minding my own business—Jill's a friend of my friend Esther—but they needed someone with a bad memory, and this is the first time it's helped anyone!

Ummm... I have about a three-to-four day range where I remember things. Before that it's just about nothing. It's mostly events, people, conversations, those sort of things. Facts are pretty bad, too, but if I understand them they have a slightly longer shelf life. Hmmm...

I don't know, I guess that's about it. I had waffles for breakfast this morning. I like waffles.

- **SCENE TWENTY-NINE (BOOK FIVE)**

SADIE carefully removes Florida's dead body from its cage and wraps it in a tea towel. She leaves the cage open and exits the stage.

- **SCENE THIRTY (BOOK THREE)**

JACK and JILL stand around the time machine. SADIE enters.

JILL: Are you ready?

SADIE: I don't know. I think so.

JACK: Is there a problem?

SADIE: It's just... I guess I don't know if I'll be any help with the records, and how many times is this going to happen, and is this helping anyone, really? And I feel a little out of myself.

JILL: Of course you're helping us, Sadie. We couldn't do any of this without you.

SADIE: I do know that.

JACK: Look, we can give you some more time if you need it. But we really need you to push that button.

JILL: Or all our research, all of our time is for naught.

JACK: And we lose the grant.

SADIE looks torn.

SADIE: Well... I guess nothing bad can come of it, right?

JILL: Absolutely.

SADIE: Well...

JILL walks SADIE to the time machine, wraps her fingers in her own, and kisses her for the first time. This comes as a shock to both SADIE and JACK.

A moment later, JILL presses their entwined fingers over the button. Snap to black.

END OF ACT TWO

ACT THREE

- **SCENE THIRTY-ONE (BOOK FIVE)**

Book Three should now be permanently closed.

SADIE sits on JILL's desk.

SADIE: I don't think I can do this.

JILL: Having cold feet?

SADIE: Freezing feet.

JILL: Well, thaw them out. You know we're doing it tonight.

SADIE: I don't think I can. I don't know, I think it was easier before—when I wasn't so happy. To just erase the world. But I don't want to lose this.

JILL: Sadie... It's just going to happen again.

SADIE: Will it? We didn't happen before.

JILL But now we have. Come and find me.

SADIE: But I don't want to lose *this*. What's happened this time. These lines on my face, the new scars on my leg, all of it. I get so happy just walking down the street, feeling the air between my fingers. I don't care if you're exactly the same back there, I want you now.

JILL: You realise you're not making sense.

SADIE: I make sense to me.

JILL: You've forgotten everything that's happened anyway.

SADIE: But it has happened. That's enough.

JILL moves to lean casually against the door.

JILL: Sadie, I need you to do this.

SADIE: Why? I've reached the highest level on the tests. You can't be any more certain than this.

JILL: But we expected you to go in the time machine.

SADIE: I know. But you knew that one day, there would be no point in my going back there. I think that's today. And if you feel like I've wasted your time, I'm sorry. I don't. You have your certainty, or as close as you're ever going to come. We both know what happened, and if it's not good enough for the rest of the scientific community then they're off their rockers.

JILL: It's not about the research, Sadie.

Silence.

It's not about you needing to go back. It's about... me... needing to go back.

SADIE: But I thought you didn't change.

JILL: No, I don't.

Silence.

SADIE: Did something happen?

JILL: What?

SADIE: Did your cat die? Your sister? Did the house burn down? What do you need to fix?

JILL: No one died.

Silence.

SADIE: I promise, you can tell me what happened. You can tell me anything. And if it's really so bad you can't tell me, then I guess I'll push the button anyway.

Silence.

JILL: The bad thing didn't happen. I did the bad thing.

SADIE: Oh.

JILL: And I knew it didn't count because we'd push the button.

SADIE: *(beat)* You won't just do it again next time, then?

JILL: I never would if I couldn't undo it.

Silence.

SADIE: You did it for free. *(beat)* You can do anything because it's not permanent.

JILL: Didn't you realise that?

SADIE: No... Well, it's not entirely un-permanent / for me.

JILL: I guess you're right. I guess it is 'free.' Especially now, when we're minutes from pushing the button, which is the only reason I'm telling you this.

SADIE: Then tell me.

SADIE kisses her.

JILL: What would you think of me?

Silence.

SADIE: Won't you always have to push it?

JILL: One day, I'll decide not to, and I won't.

SADIE: But you'll always want to. Whatever it is you did.

JILL: No, maybe not. I haven't before.

Silence.

SADIE: Me? *(beat)* You built a time machine so you could fuck me for free?

JILL: God!

SADIE: That's what you want to erase?

JILL: Don't flatter yourself! I didn't build the thing for you!

SADIE: Oh, so just for everyone?!

JILL: *(beat)* What? No! I didn't know it would make me forget. I only found that out later.

SADIE is in tears.

SADIE: So it's still a secret and you don't care.

JILL: We're not all like you, Sadie. We can't just do whatever and forget two days later. Some of us have to live with ourselves.

SADIE: I have to live with myself!

JILL: You barely open your journals.

SADIE: That doesn't mean a thing! You think I'm not ashamed? Count my shame in every goddamn word! I live / with myself.

JILL: Then understand I want to take it away.

Silence.

SADIE: You're ashamed of me.

JILL: I lived this entire rewind for you.

SADIE: Which you're gonna erase.

JILL:	Because when I do it for real, it's going to be nothing. You don't have any idea. Even if I tell you, you'll forget. Because you only get one chance and it has to be perfect but it never is. I just wanted to make something to get it right. And when it couldn't be right, I just wanted a chance to get it wrong! How exhausting to be right all the time. How tiring, to make your pupils small and your hands clasp. To wear a mouth-guard every night so your teeth don't grind to stumps. Your skin's so soft! Like you've never lived a day in your life. Don't worry about yesterday or tomorrow; you'll forget. Just a little bit of time before I die. Just a little bit of time I built myself, is that too much to ask? Just a little bit of time where time means nothing, where I don't have to worry, where it's going to be okay!
SADIE:	Jill, it's going to be okay.
JILL:	No.
SADIE:	You haven't done anything. Everything's fine. You can do fine with this.
JILL:	No.
SADIE:	I'm not going to push the button just so you can forget being with me.
JILL:	No.
SADIE:	Erasing this isn't going to make it any better. If you want to be with me, then you should just be with me. If you go back you'll just feel worse.

JILL hurries out of the room, SADIE following behind her.

In front of them, JACK stands beside the time machine.

JILL:	Sadie's not going to push it.
JACK:	Why not?
JILL:	She doesn't want to start again.

JACK: But it's going to be better next time. It's always better because of what you learn.

SADIE: But I like this time.

JACK: But next time will be better.

SADIE: I don't want it to be better.

JACK: I'm sorry you're upset, Sadie. But you always knew you'd push the button. You agreed to that very clearly. You're not going to waste our last six months because you refuse to go back and live them better.

SADIE: I'm not wasting them!

JACK: No, not if you push the button.

JILL: Come on, I've had enough of this.

SADIE: *(to Jack)* There's no more research to be done! You're not going to find anything else! You're never going to crack a way to properly send things back in six months. This six months. This goddamn six months! Why do you want to send me back?

JACK: The research isn't over.

SADIE: Yes it is!

JACK: *(to Jill)* She's hysterical. What happened?

SADIE lunges for the time machine. She gets one arm around it as JACK grabs her.

JACK: Sadie! What's gotten into you? For God's sake. Well, push the button.

SADIE: No! I have to live with this!

JACK tries to lean over her to reach the button. She holds it out of his reach.

JACK: Jill, what's going on?

SADIE: Why do you want me to do this? Are you fucking someone, too? / I don't understand.

JACK: What the / hell?

JILL: Sadie!

SADIE elbows JACK in the face—hard and sharp. He lets her go. She runs to the door, time machine in her arms, but JILL's there already.

SADIE: So it can never be over. Do you realise that? The research never stops for him, it can never be over, because if it's over what happens? Nothing. Nothing can ever be proven, nothing can ever come of this. He knows, he knows. You're always going to do this. 'Round and 'round and 'round, never perfect, always wrong because he'll always push the button, even if you've done it right this time. Even if you don't want to.

JILL: But you'll be different.

SADIE: But who the fuck cares?

JILL: Because it'll be different.

SADIE: Let me out. Let me out!

JACK: If you don't stop right now I'm calling the cops.

JILL: *(to Sadie)* No, you're right. Let's do this right.

SADIE tries to kick JILL, but the time machine makes it awkward and JILL catches her leg and wrenches it up, throwing SADIE to the ground.

JILL: Sorry.

JILL grabs the time machine.

         Remember that.

JILL slams her hand into the button.

Snap to black.

- **SCENE THIRTY-TWO (BOOK SIX)**

All three original notebooks are now permanently shut.

A fourth notebook lands at Sadie's feet. It looks different: she's chosen this one herself.

SADIE: I met Esther's friend Jill today. So noteworthy it actually warranted buying this new journal, fancy that. In any case, Jill just sauntered up and interrupted our coffee, and I felt so ill I had to excuse myself to the toilets. I don't know why I found her so repulsive. By the time I came back she was gone. Esther says she's okay but I'm usually right about people. Took a while for the sick to go away. I feel alright now. Oh well—I'll forget her tomorrow.

END

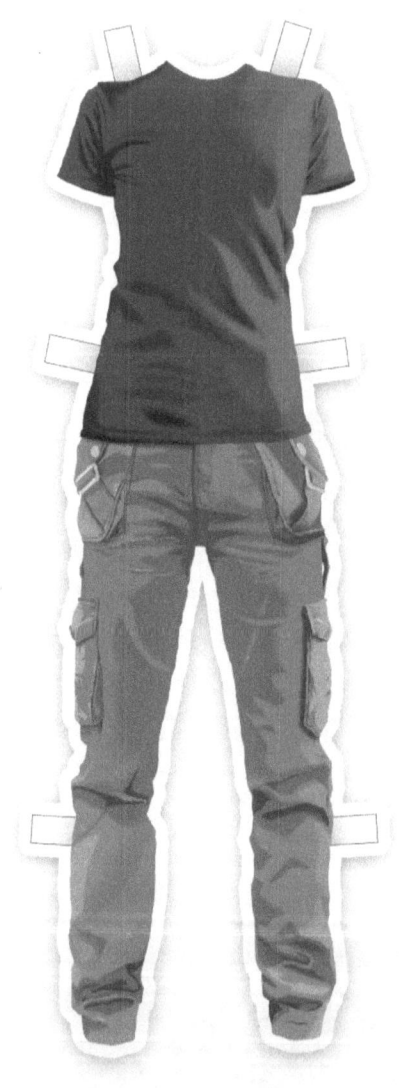

BACK FROM FAIRY LAND

CHARACTERS:

MADALYN WALKER: A visitor to fairy land.

SETTING:

The stage of an innovation conference. Victoria, Australia. The present.

ACT ONE

An innovation conference. MADALYN WALKER (14) stands alone on stage, in the middle of a clear cube (glass or plastic) which is slightly over two metres long on each side. She wears a headset mic, a nice t-shirt, cargo pants and boots.

MADALYN: Hi, everyone.

Um, my name is Madalyn, and in case you don't know I'm here to talk to you because I came back from fairy land recently.

That's, uh, that's just what everyone's calling it to me—it has an actual name that's just difficult to pronounce—but they call this world, here, The Land That Light Forgot, so I've been calling over there Lightworld.

I know a lot of people still don't believe that I was there at all, so I'm grateful I get to talk to you today. I mean, I'm not trying to advertise this, it's just that 18 different people with phones and eyes are hard to ignore. It just worked out that way. And if everyone knows the story anyway I don't want them to think I'm making it all up.

The story is this: I was camping at Wilson's Prom with my mum and dad, and a big group of us decided to go rambling. I think that's more of a British term, but you guys get it. We went rambling, and uh, one of my favourite things is trying to fit myself between rocks. We'd paused because someone thought they'd seen a wallaby, and everyone had their phones on video. I didn't much care about the wallaby and after a minute my dad stopped caring, too, so he turns to me and says, "Don't get yourself stuck, Maddie," because I'm kinda fitting myself in between these two rocks. And then everyone's turning around to see if I get stuck.

But I don't get stuck because I vanish between the rocks and I'm gone. And my dad drops his phone and runs towards where I was, but the rocks don't go anywhere, there's no hole, there's just rocks. And two minutes and 21 seconds later, I reappear from nowhere, and there are half a dozen videos of the whole thing.

And Lightworld—well, I'm here to tell you about fairy land.

I was actually over there for about 12 days—their time. And it's beautiful over there. Anything beautiful over here is like a six-year-old trying to copy a van Gogh painting. *(pause)* By which I mean, you can get the general impression, but it's not really like the beauty over there at all.

I woke up alone, in a tower. Everything was dusty but the bed was made.

MADALYN picks up an orange marker from a small table in the corner of the box. She starts to draw the outside of the tower on the front wall of the cube.

It was sunset, and there were fireflies everywhere. There was a pile of identical maps on the table, held down with stones, with 'you are here' and a map of the surrounding area. And carved into the wood of the door to the staircase, were some instructions:

(singsong) This bed is your portal
If you're hurrying home
Take nothing back
And bring a map
If you go outside alone

Underneath that, I think the same message was written in Chinese, but I only took Chinese for one semester two years ago.

As you might have guessed, I left the tower.

I know you're probably expecting me to have gone on a quest or gotten in terrible trouble or something, but I was only there for 12 days and the world didn't seem to need saving or anything. I mean, it has its good and bad points, but it trundles along just like ours. And I already knew how to get home. And that I couldn't stay too long, because my family and friends would be worried about me.

So mostly, I was just a tourist.

We don't have all day so let me just tell you some of it.

She's been trying to act restrained and professional up to this point, but now her excitement bursts through.

They have these tattoos, over there, where they infuse the ink with light and put it under the skin, so people glow with moonlight or sunlight or something coming out of them. And there are groups called shoreliners who have most of their bodies done up like this and camp near bodies of water, and they swim at night like lantern fish and catch sea creatures to eat. There were octopuses who built cities at the bottom of lakes. The capital city of Lightworld is called The Melting City, because it's all made of glass and I learnt that glass is actually a liquid that just runs incredibly slowly. The Melting City floats all over the world. It's on this bubble of air. I didn't get on it because it could have floated miles away and I needed to get home, but I'm told the Queen of Sunrise lives there. There are Children of Lightning who grow on trees and hatch when the lightning hits. There are flowers that look like long, thin tulips that grant you a vision of the future when picked. There's a ballroom with a mirrored floor which reflects all your flaws to everyone.

Quickly, with the orange marker, she draws a simple room with a person standing on the floor. Their reflection stretches out like a shadow: clear with dark patches of flaws.

I did two kinds of apprenticeships over there, for food and a place to sleep. The first was in The Terrible Kitchen. The ladies in there mostly bake and are usually naked with just aprons on top. They take things out of dead creatures and humans like courage or musical skill or the ability to breathe underwater, and they bake those things into their bread and cupcakes and friends. It freaked me out at first, but they were all really nice and it was always warm in there and they said I could come back whenever I liked. When I left, they gave me a bunch of food tied up in a jellyfish balloon. It's like they contain helium but you can tie and untie them and fill them with barbeque-flavoured bravery scrolls.

The second place I worked was this barn surrounded by circus tents. I mean, there weren't any circus folk in them, but I think they'd been used as that at one stage. They use these things like hang-gliders *(she draws one)* where you lie flat and cycle the pedals. It makes the wings flap, and if you take off from an appropriate point you can fly around in the sky for a good half hour!

What they're looking for are secret beetles. Secret beetles bite you and learn something you've never told anyone. Then, if you catch them and eat their insides, you get the secret.

She glances at the clock on the far wall, behind the audience, and sighs.

I'm running out of time and I haven't even told you about the candlelighters and The Suicide Forest. But that's okay because there's next time.

In case you didn't know, you can see in your programmes I'm coming back to speak twice more. In a couple of days, and then in a couple more days. Because they're sending me back to Lightworld two more times. I'll get to see more of everything and maybe fly the Gear Wings again.

Before I go, I'm going to answer some of your questions which were collected earlier.

She picks up an electronic tablet from the small table in corner.

"Did you eat anything over there?"

Yes, I did. I'd still die if I didn't eat.

She flicks to the next question on the tablet.

"What did you bring back?"

Nothing, unfortunately. I tried to bring back the map and a magical scarf I got from the beetle hunters, but they wouldn't go through. You're not allowed to take anything with you. It's like a national park.

"Did you meet anyone else from our world over there?"

I don't think so, but there must be others. Why would that tower room exist? Someone from our world has prepared it for more visitors. *(pause)* I mean, I'm not the first girl to disappear from some Australian rocks.

"Is anyone from fairy land planning to come to our world? Do you think they might declare war?"

Um, no, not at all. They'd find that really funny. They think this world is like a giant pile of trash. Like, not even the good kind of trash you can burn for fuel. They have zero interest in us.

Um, I think that's the end of the questions and I'm out of time. So I might see you next time after I've been to Lightworld again. Thank you.

Lights down.

END OF ACT ONE

ACT TWO

Lights up on MADALYN WALKER. She still looks 14, and still stands inside the clear cube. She may have changed her hair or her t-shirt, but everything else is the same as we left it.

MADALYN: It's so strange to be back here. *(She runs a finger next to her old drawings)* In this 14-year-old body. In this world where everything is so obvious. Things do just what they were meant to do. A chair is just a chair. A coat is just a coat.

It's very weird looking in the mirror and seeing a child. A tallish child with breasts. I'm sure I didn't think of myself as a child at 14. I'm 10 years older now, so... probably still a child to most of you. I know 10 years is longer than I was supposed to have stayed. Even if it was only about 10 hours, your time. My parents worried. It's good to see them. But life catches on to you as you get older. You have responsibilities. I had friends over there. I almost had a family. I had a briar fox. You have to pick the right time to up and leave everything.

Early on in my second stay, I got stuck in The Suicide Forest. We call it that because nothing will hunt you there. Nothing is hidden and deadly. But there are lots of dangerous things right out in the open, waiting for anyone sad or stupid or careless enough to run into them.

I was working for the Keepery, flying a Gear Wing, chasing a secret beetle. I'd been away hundreds of years before returning and some things were different and some were the same. I was 15 and much too confident. Anyway, I got my leg snagged on a greyhaze thorn vine. The thorns are like this... *(she draws one, the size of her hand)* This size. Life size. Not good. Now, aside from being giant and painful these also cause almost instant paralysis. So I fell out of the sky, to the floor of The Suicide Forest, feet still tangled in the pedals. And I knew enough to know that it wasn't the fall that would kill me. It wasn't the blood loss. It was the briar foxes. They're attracted to the smell of the greyhaze poison mixed with blood. I could barely move. And I could see one slinking out of the bushes.

One of my arms still half-worked. So I stretched into my backpack for some dumplings and sweet breads and tossed them to the fox.

Well, she ate through my entire backpack, but she was mine after that. And she waited for me to recover and rode on my shoulders and I called her Sweetling.

There are two things you should know about briar foxes. The first is that if you run your fingers enough through their fur, gems will fall out. Diamonds behind the ears and sapphires behind the ankles and rubies at the belly. The second thing is that they can fly. And they can carry six times their weight when they do it, like an ant.

So one of the reasons I came back was because Sweetling was getting old, and sick. I went back to the tower that houses the portal, and the door was shut. I couldn't open it. I don't know, maybe it only opens for human children. So I hung onto Sweetling and she flew us up to the tower window. We stayed there for the last two weeks of her life. I read her stories and fed her treats. And then she died. And I came here.

I'm not going to stay here long, though. I have responsibilities there.

She picks up the tablet.

Question time.

"What do they call their world, in fairy land?"

(writing it on the wall) Min-ell-loh-thi.

"Has anyone gone in after you? Has the military sent anyone through the portal?"

No, to the best of my knowledge no one else has been able to pass through since I went through the first time.

"Why is The Terrible Kitchen called terrible?"

I didn't know for a long time, either. But things weren't always so peaceful. They used to bake things like sickness and despair into their food, in wartimes. For the enemy, obviously. I hear a lot of innovation comes with war.

"Did you get any tattoos with light in them?"

They're called inklight tattoos, and yes, I had firelight ones all down my legs. I miss them. Makes it hard to sleep without them covered up, though. The light wakes you up.

"Did you go to The Melting City?"

Yes, I lived there for the last four and a half years.

"Did you go back to the ballroom with the mirrored floors?"

I did. They hold annual masquerade balls there, for those who can get in. I met my ex-husband there. You can't see anyone's faces but you can see all their flaws right there spread out on the floor. We broke up not long ago. He never really understood my responsibilities. Didn't understand my coming back here. So just knowing each other's flaws does not a relationship save. But it was good while it lasted.

"Did you pick the flowers that gave you a vision of the future?"

Yes.

"Did you ever learn a secret from the secret beetles?"

That was my job for most of the time, in one way or another. So I've learnt hundreds of secrets. The trick is knowing who the secret belongs to. Because you get a lot of secrets that are useless without an owner.

But if you can lock someone alone in a room with a secret beetle, then you get some of the best results.

A brief silence.

The secrets are classified into four tiers by the keepers.

First are the ones that no one cares about. Like seven-year-old Crockett is allergic to pine nuts.

Second are the ones someone cares about, and will give you a bit of money for. Like 15-year-old Crockett is allergic to pine nuts and a classmate wants him out of the school play.

Third tier are the ones someone cares about and will give you a lot of money for, like the queen is allergic to pine nuts.

And the fourth and highest tier: secrets that everyone cares about. Like Crockett murdered the queen last week with a handful of pine nuts.

Last question.

"What aren't you telling us?"

(laughs) I was there for 10 years. So almost everything.

Lights down.

END OF ACT TWO

ACT THREE

Lights up on MADALYN WALKER. Days have passed, but everything is still the same as we left it. MADALYN still has her cargo pants and boots on, but her top and hair look rough and thrown together.

MADALYN: Every second counts. We need your help. There is a war, and it will destroy everything. My family. My children. Everything over there will be annihilated.

You know the real reason no one else can go over there. The portal wants children. Sixteen and under. Please, lend us your children. They will have wild adventures. They will be heroes. They will not come to much harm; the creatures attacking us have no interest in humans.

You understand how time works over there. Please, lend me your children. I'll have them home before dinner.

Silence.

Why are you sitting there silently, when every moment means more of my people die?

More information. They come through a portal much like this one, and they eat light magic. They're not evil, but they're animalistic. They feed. And many of my people are held together with magic. Take it away, and there's nothing left. The rest of them are weak and confused. It takes a while for them to learn how to live without magic. Like losing your legs. This is why humans are important. They're not targets. They can't lose their light. They can fight back.

I left my people, my family, in crisis to come here. To bring back help. I wouldn't ask if it wasn't dire.

> *(laughs)* I am not used to being met with such disregard. Perhaps I was naive. Do you simply not care? Mum and Dad, you have no interest in the survival of your grandchildren? How silly of me to have forgotten.

MADALYN approaches the door at the back of the clear cube. She tries to let herself out, but the door is locked tightly. She spends several seconds trying to open it.

> Release me.
>
> Release me at once! I will not have everyone die due to a locked door!

She stands in the middle of the cube, facing the audience.

> I am Her Royal Highness Madalyn Walker, Sunset Queen, Empress of Minellothi, Ruler of the Melting City. I wear the great tentacles of Arranthorn around my neck and the light of the Flame of the World inside my belly. You will show me respect!

By force of habit, she throws out her arms to either side of herself, forgetting that magic doesn't work here.

Slowly, panting, she realises that nothing has happened.

> Please. While there is still time. Please.

Silence. Several moments pass.

> You realise you have just condemned a whole world to death.

She sinks to the floor. Eventually, she picks up the orange marker from the table, and starts to colour in the clear wall between her and the audience with big, rough strokes.

> Last time I came here... *(correcting herself)* Just before—I was pregnant. It didn't come across. I was thankful. It wasn't time. I had to be queen one day. I wasn't ready for that. I was supposed to kill her, the Sunrise Queen. When she found out, she was glad. She'd seen the future, with the war. She wanted a boring little

girl like me: no magic. She'd been ruling too long, she
was tired. But I thought I was too young and ignorant, so
I said wait. Wait just a little longer, just a couple more
decades, and I'll come back. I'll be fourteen and you can
teach me everything I need to know. I'll keep the world
safe.

I kissed her before I killed her, and she said: keep
everyone safe.

I have a sister over there, Mom and Dad. I found her in
the Labyrinth of Lost Things. My twin that died in your
belly when I didn't. Not many make it through the
labyrinth, but I did. I did a lot of things. Good and bad.
And stupid things.

Silence.

Do you really think I'm only 14 years old? I've lived 74.

Silence.

When you eat people's secrets you learn how terrible they
are. You dance with their flaws and think how awful.
How wasteful. How cowardly. But then, in a corner of the
ballroom, there's someone whose flaws you gather up.
You gather them up to your chest and stroke them. You
tell them bedtime stories and that everything is going to
be okay.

You tell your wife that you'll go through the portal, and
leave everyone alone. But it'll be worth it.

She studies the clock on the wall, behind the audience.

Even if you changed your minds right now, it's too late.
Too much time will have passed over there. They'll have
almost certainly lost.

*By now, she is standing. There is not much of the front wall of the cube
left to colour. She pauses while the audience can still see her face.*

When *I* saw the future, I saw myself leading an army of human children across the plains of Minellothi, and I thought that would be now. It's not now, but it will be soon. You won't give them, but I will take them from you. Dozens of children through the portal. You won't keep me away. I drunk it, the very first time I was over there. The pomegranate juice. On the desk, in the tower. It won't let me stay away for long.

And most children, they won't be as generous as I was. They won't come back at all.

After all, what is there for them here?

Madalyn finishes colouring in the front wall of the cube, so that the audience can no longer see her clearly. She turns her back.

Lights down.

END

TETHER

CHARACTERS (in order of appearance):

GEORGIA: An aspiring businesswoman.
JOHN: A filmmaker.
STEVE: A comedian.
CLAIRE: A biology student.
DAWN: A parish secretary.
AUGUST: A charity worker.
VALERIE: An art gallery manager.
MAX: A student.
FI: A homemaker.
CHRIS: A businessman.

SETTING:

Melbourne, Australia. The present.

A NOTE ON FORMATTING:

A forward slash (/) is used to indicate when the next character begins speaking before the first character has finished their line(s). Wherever a forward slash appears inside a character's dialogue, the next character should begin to say their line(s) immediately. This will lead to two characters speaking at the same time for at least a moment; this is wholly intentional and is mandatory for all productions.

- **SCENE ONE**

GEORGIA (22) slumps on the couch. JOHN (24) stands a few metres away, holding a handheld video camera. He is parodying documentaries.

JOHN: And here sits the extrovert, in all her Sunday night glory, doing absolutely nothing.

GEORGIA: John...

JOHN: Humans are group animals, and this is particularly embodied in the extroverted subsection. Some scientists say their nervous system is naturally sluggish, and requires regular excitement to jolt it into a balanced place.

GEORGIA: *(warning)* If I didn't want to be distracted...

JOHN: Thus, the extrovert will accept any sort of excitement over sitting alone.

GEORGIA: If anyone sees this tape, I will never talk to you again.

John flicks the camera into standby.

JOHN: I'm trying to make a point here, Georgia.

GEORGIA: What? The 'Georgia's alone and depressed' point? Because that's not true, and don't you try and twist it.

JOHN: No. That's not what I'm trying to say at all. *(beat)* I'm trying to say that everyone's alone and depressed.

GEORGIA leaps to her feet and tries to steal the camera from JOHN. He wins their brief grapple.

JOHN: See. You don't really give a shit about my movie. You just want the excitement of arguing with me.

GEORGIA: Oh, believe me, I care about not coming off as a loser to whoever ends up watching that.

JOHN: Fine. I won't show anyone. Just answer this.

JOHN flicks the camera on again.

JOHN: Why are you alone tonight?

SCENE TWO

STEVE (21) knocks on Claire's door.

STEVE: Hey. You in there? Gem said you barely left your room all week. I guess they're worried.

CLAIRE (19) opens the door. A bit dishevelled but otherwise fine.

CLAIRE: For goodness sake. Hello, Steve. Come in. Can't a girl have some time to herself sometimes?

They enter Claire's room.

STEVE: What's up, girl?

CLAIRE: Just doing some research.

STEVE: Yeah?

CLAIRE: On holes. *(beat)* Here. *(she points to her heart)*

STEVE: Right. This a physical or emotional thing?

CLAIRE shakes her head.

STEVE: Well, that's good... At least you're not dying.

CLAIRE marks a page in a Biology textbook with a sticky-note, then shuts the book.

CLAIRE: Know anything about stem cells?

STEVE: Some. They can change into any other cell type, right? That's why they're being researched so much. We can change them into useful shit. *(beat)* You need stem cells?

CLAIRE: No. More... We *are* all stem cells. I mean, we can be anything. We can change into anything. There's no prior determination. We're all free to be and do anything we like.

STEVE: Yeah. Sure.

CLAIRE: Except... stem cells don't really choose what they change into. They pick the sort of cell the body needs. But us? We don't have anything to take reference from. I'm trying to figure out why we should choose anything; there's no reason to make one choice over another. It seems like... we don't have any real reason to do anything any more.

- **SCENE THREE**

JOHN sets up his camera on a tripod in front of DAWN (25). He fiddles for a couple of seconds, then turns it on and exits.

DAWN: People talk about the fall of organised religion. After the Second World War. Like religion's gone and we're now in an atheist era.

And firstly, I think, that's rubbish, because clearly we're still around and we make our presence known, I think. And secondly, how depressing for everyone. I look at all these people who don't believe, and there's so much they're missing out on. My life would be so different, so much less rich without my faith.

I wouldn't call it the fall of organised religion. That sounds like religion's tripped and cracked its head open. Rather, I'd call it a minor exodus. Like lemmings. You know, the little furry creatures that jump off the cliff. Maybe that's better. It was the jump of organised religion.

My parents were Christians and we went to church twice every Sunday. When I was really young it was a tradition. I didn't have a personal relationship with God until I was a bit older and the pastor explained we needed to choose, that we needed to make our own personal decision. It was the best one I ever made.

I get a little sick of everyone asking, "If God's so good, why does he let terrible things happen." You have to have faith in God. Faith is the most important thing. If you can't stick around when your faith is tested... then you become one of them, out there. So many of their lives just seem like a string of distractions.

And I just thank God that I don't need any of that. That I have everything I need through Him.

I'm going to make cupcakes for the church fete on Sunday. You should come along. Everyone's family there.

- **SCENE FOUR**

GEORGIA and AUGUST (25) on a coffee break:

AUGUST: My mother's overseas. Country starting with 'D'... What'cha thinking? Denmark? Everyone always thinks Denmark. It is Denmark. My father's in England. They split up when I was 15. My sister lives with my mother. We're exact opposites. We don't talk much. My stepbrother distanced himself from us before I moved out. I send him a letter every month. I never get a reply.

GEORGIA: You've done everything you can.

AUGUST: Yeah. It's not really me I'm worried about, it's him. What about you? What about your family?

GEORGIA: Well... my parents are both in the country. But both their extended families are overseas, so I've never really understood the concept of family, I guess. Only child.

AUGUST: Yeah... Fuckin' global village.

GEORGIA: Global village?

AUGUST: I mean, it's a joke, isn't it? We can go anywhere we want. It's just a plane trip away. We're all separated. No one really has their family together any more. We're all just blobs. Alone. Little flicks of light, flitting around. When you have your family nearby you have some sort of identity. Now everyone just sticks things to themselves to gather some sort of... compensation for the soul. Sense of belonging. Buy a Porsche, you're a guy who bought a Porsche. You know?

GEORGIA: Flypaper for the soul?

AUGUST: Ha. Yeah.

GEORGIA: I wouldn't always want to be identified by my family, though. I mean, I do want to escape who I... represent to them. Get my own life. My own freedom.

AUGUST: Everyone does. It's just that freedom comes at a price. Not any better or worse. Just the resulting good and bad. I mean, it's like letting a helium balloon go. It's free. Blissful, terrible freedom. Am I right?

- **SCENE FIVE**

VALERIE (37) sits in front of JOHN's video camera.

VALERIE: I'm going to remind you again, I'm only doing this because you're promising to blur out my face. I still think people will recognise my voice. I only agree if I'm utterly anonymous. I'd ask someone else to say this, instead of me, but then it wouldn't come out right. So I guess it has to be me, and I trust you to fix it up properly.

This year, I'm going to celebrate my thirtieth birthday again. And the first time I celebrated it was a few years after I turned 30, so maybe you get an idea of my age. I can still pull it off, so why not, if I still look and feel that young?

But basically, I'm running out of time to have children. And when I say I won't be having them, people have stopped correcting me. So I'm sort of on a tightrope here. There's no man. There's only me. And I don't even have a cat to look after, so there's no way I could handle a baby alone.

And someone asked me the other day... Asked me why I wanted one in the first place. I mean, women don't have to have them these days. It's not all about marriage and kids and the white picket fence.

Except it is. It still is. No, I won't be socially ostracised for being barren and alone. I'm only answerable to myself. But myself still yells, in my mind, you're alone in your apartment and you don't even have a cat! And you're going to die ugly and alone and no one will care about you or need you any more.

So you see why you need to blur out my face now. Don't you, John. You better buy me a bunch of flowers for this verbal vomit I've given you.

- **SCENE SIX**

MAX (22) and AUGUST, on phones:

MAX: So what I want to know is, why is it so bad? I mean, why can't I just have sex with people?

AUGUST: I don't know? 'Cos they don't say yes?

MAX: Oh, they always say yes. I mean, why isn't it okay for me to be a man-whore?

AUGUST: Maybe because you use the word man-whore.

MAX: Seriously, though. I have a lot of sex. Is that a bad thing? Really?

AUGUST: Absolutely not. You have your sex. Sex is good. Live it up, I say.

MAX: Thank you! Not that I would've stopped either way.

AUGUST: Some people just find it confronting. They expect sex to mean something. But of course, these are the people who give value to everything.

MAX: Sex has value.

AUGUST: I mean, they expect it to have some sort of profound meaning to you.

MAX: Like hell it does! That's why I can have so much of it.

AUGUST: If they didn't expect it to have some intrinsic meaning, they wouldn't care how much you got.

MAX: You really think they're so holier-than-thou, simply because they can't stand the thought that this, this 'precious' thing is as meaningless as anything else?

AUGUST: I think that's exactly why.

They both hang up their phones, meet in the space between them and start to make out.

MAX: Their loss, then.

AUGUST: Come on, my housemates are out 'til seven.

- **SCENE SEVEN**

FI (25) sits in front of JOHN's video camera.

FI: I used to think I was born in the wrong decade. Maybe wrong century. I mean, all that tradition, the stereotypes really appeal to me. You knew exactly what you were supposed to do back then. Be a good wife, cook the dinner, shine your husband's shoes, all of that. Always seemed really sweet to me. People stick their noses up at it, say we didn't have any choices back then and we were all really oppressed. And I understand those arguments, I do. But... a lack of choice, that's also freeing. It's like giving children school uniforms. They don't have to think about what they're going to wear in the morning.

People talk about freedom everywhere now. If you're aware of it, you hear it everywhere. Much more than I used to hear it. I don't know what's changed in our culture lately, maybe people are feeling powerless due to the global financial climate and global warming and other disasters with 'global' in them.

And every time people talk about freedom, they always assume it's something people want.

Freedom's a funny word. These days, it seems to mean only being answerable to yourself. But not everyone wants that sort of responsibility. It's much easier just doing what you're told. You don't have to worry about doing the right thing. You know you're doing it right.

I don't want to be free, if that's what freedom means. That's exhausting.

Actually, I have a great story for you, but I can't say it on tape.

She grins sheepishly.

Maybe just imagine it.

- **SCENE EIGHT**

JOHN adjusts the video camera while CHRIS (34) takes a seat in front of it.

CHRIS: I don't really understand what I'm supposed to do.

JOHN: Just talk to the camera.

CHRIS: I'm not an idiot, John. But I can't talk about 'Meaning, Loneliness and Freedom' for more than the five seconds it takes to tell you it's a bunch of horseshit.

JOHN: Then talk about other people.

CHRIS: Anything more specific?

JOHN: Nope. Not if I don't want you to bite my head off. Go for it.

JOHN turns on the video camera and exits.

CHRIS: Let's be clear. Other people. They exist. I have a wife. She's pretty. I have a company. They're useful. I have some friends, like John, who I occasionally do dumb favours for, because they let me complain to them when I need to debrief, because someone else is being an arsehole.

Generally, other people take up space. They're not as smart as me, they're not as rich as me, and they don't have as much cool stuff as I have. Today, I'm bored. I'm going to buy another car and see whether I feel any better.

Is that what you wanted, John? Yeah, screw you.

SCENE NINE

GEORGIA and STEVE on Steve's bed:

STEVE: So I got the gig! I'm going to be a stand-up comic! Professionally!

GEORGIA: That's fantastic!

STEVE: I know! I mean, I feel like I'm finally making it.

GEORGIA: You've worked really hard.

STEVE: Yeah. If I can just make one person laugh, it's worth it, you know? I feel like I'm making a difference.

GEORGIA: We'll call you Patch Adams.

Silence. STEVE suddenly looks pensive.

GEORGIA: Look, you can't help everyone. You can't put that sort of burden on yourself. You're not responsible for their welfare.

STEVE: Sure I am. We're all responsible for everyone's welfare. As soon as they all wake up and realise that, the world will start to fix itself.

GEORGIA: I'm talking about one person in particular.

STEVE: Well, you do what you can. She seems to be getting worse now, but she goes up and down.

GEORGIA: Oh? What's it now?

STEVE: She wants to be religious, but she can't be because she thinks it's bullshit.

GEORGIA: Oh. Well, you're not responsible for dealing with that. That's her issue. Lord knows we each have enough ourselves already. No pun intended.

STEVE: Fail. *(beat)* I mean it, though. Everyone's so out for themselves. Like anything they do for them is going to make them happy. It's ironic but it's true. I'm not going to be happy until I can make Claire laugh.

GEORGIA: Good luck, mate.

- **SCENE TEN**

CLAIRE and AUGUST are playing with blocks, scales, butcher's paper and markers.

JOHN stands a few metres away with his handheld camera.

JOHN: 3.32 pm. The emo and the hippy revisit their childhood by playing with blocks from August's attic.

CLAIRE: Hey! I'm not an emo! Bastard.

JOHN: *(laughs)* Tell the nice people what you're doing.

AUGUST: We are attempting to measure the optimum level of freedom. The scale goes from Buffy, who is responsible for everyone in the face of countless apocalypses, to, well, people like me.

JOHN: *(affectionately)* You slut!

AUGUST: Yes, lovely, John. You're a very funny man.

CLAIRE: It has to do with how heavy people are. Too heavy, and you drown. Too light, you float away. Depends on how many tethers are pulling you to earth. The optimum level seems to be submerged with your head above water.

AUGUST: Makes sense, lovely.

CLAIRE: The light people tend to try to make a lot of connections... Some bring them down to earth. Some don't help them at all. Sometimes you don't have any viable tethers to connect to yourself. I don't have school any more, and I don't want family or religion, and people tend to piss me off, so... I don't know. I'm trying to find an alternative so I don't float away.

AUGUST: She has a project. As long as she has a project, she'll be okay.

JOHN: You may have just made my video.

AUGUST: Not bad for an emo and a hippy, huh?

- **SCENE ELEVEN**

MAX sits in front of JOHN's video camera.

MAX: Everyone takes life much too seriously. We don't have to. You're born, you've got a few years to soak up as much of life as you can and you die. That's it. So if you're not grabbing as much of it as you possibly can, that's pretty wasteful.

    I'm never wasteful. Give me just as much laughter, women and good times as I can handle without killing myself. It's not being greedy—it's being appreciative. People who throw away their lives being sad deserve what they get.

    And I know what you're going to say, John. "It's all an act, Max. You're not really like that. You're just being arrogant to cover up your own insecurities."

    No! This isn't an act. This is me. This is what I *believe*. We're all gonna die so we've all gotta live in the meantime. Life's a game, you know, and I always win at games.

    So come on—who wants a ride on the Max-mobile?

- **SCENE TWELVE**

Inside Fi's kitchen:

DAWN: So, are you religious?

FI: Oh. No. Not really. I mean, I love religions, but I'm not religious, no.

DAWN: I'm not sure I quite follow.

FI: I think they're lovely. And useful. And wonderfully traditional.

FI hands DAWN a mug of tea.

DAWN: Thank you. How are they... useful?

FI: Why, they keep everyone together. And happy. Just like floral wallpaper, aren't they?

DAWN: Well, I wouldn't exactly say that. Do you go to church?

FI: Christmas and Easter. Really, I should go more, but as I said, I'm not really religious. I just find it heart-warming. All of the lovely people and the singing and everything.

DAWN: I see.

FI: It's like a fuzzy blanket for the soul.

DAWN: Yes.

FI: I'd go Sunday mornings, but I always make pancakes then, and do two loads of washing, and make the birthday cards for the week and post them, and do some Yogalates, and I couldn't possibly fit all of that in any other time of the week. You understand.

DAWN: Well, it's all a matter of sacrifice and priorities.

FI: Oh, yes! I mean, none of us are happy without sacrifice, are we? If we don't sacrifice something else then what we choose isn't worth anything.

CHRIS enters via the front door.

CHRIS: Honey, I'm home!

FI beams and kisses him.

▪ SCENE THIRTEEN

GEORGIA sits in front of John's video camera.

GEORGIA: I read a lot of self-help books. Not because I think there's anything major wrong with me... I'm just spiritually ambitious. I think that's what irritates me about so much of the population. Their spiritual laziness. They don't reflect on anything significant about themselves and they're definitely not striving for betterment. I mean, isn't that important? That we're the best people we can be? Is it only me that thinks this?

Anyway, I read a lot of self-help books. I have to be in the right mood, but I'm trying to get there, you know. To be successful. To win at life. And I've been thinking about what that means, you know. Because it's largely subjective, and there's no banner that falls from the sky, and there aren't any angels appearing to trumpet your victory. "Congratulations, you have won. You may now die happy!"

Yeah, I'm a bit of a geek. Sorry. You can cut that bit if you want.

And I don't have the answers, really. Except that I think you win when you're happy. When you're satisfied, whatever that takes.

And now I'm thinking, maybe people are spiritually lazy, but maybe they're satisfied anyway, and maybe that makes it okay. If they're happy with their life if they should be hit by a flaming toilet seat flying out of the sky tomorrow.

Silence.

You know what, John? I really think we should scrap this. I should've never agreed in the first place, I'm sorry. People might know what my honest opinion was. Can't have that. Might be going into politics. I mean, that's why most things have happened in my life—people make political choices and I end up alone.

Okay, now you really need to cut. I will kill you if you keep this in, John.

Silence.

> I'm not terribly spiritually evolved, am I?

- **SCENE FOURTEEN**

Inside Dawn's church:

DAWN: Well, this is a pleasant surprise.

VALERIE: I saw your plans for an art display of some sort. I carved out a bit of time, thought I might help out.

DAWN: That's very kind of you! That's what you do, isn't it, things with art?

VALERIE: Uhhh, in a gallery, yes. That's where I work.

DAWN: Well, we'd be thrilled to have you on board.

VALERIE: Wonderful.

DAWN: Do you do much volunteer work?

VALERIE: I used to do a lot, before work started to get too hectic. I really want to start again. I mean, it's supposed to be really good for the soul, isn't it? I always feel better when I'm helping people. Gives you a helper's high? *(laughs)* That's the scientific term.

DAWN: Well, we always do a lot of volunteer work, and we're happy here, so I'm inclined to agree.

VALERIE: I don't think you can feel fulfilled without making some sort of difference.

DAWN: Do you not do that through the art gallery?

VALERIE: Oh... Well, sometimes, if I'm lucky.

Silence.

Where can I start?

- **SCENE FIFTEEN**

STEVE and CLAIRE in Claire's bedroom:

STEVE: What do you have against other people?

CLAIRE: They're... Everything. I have everything against them.

STEVE: I can't understand what you mean if you keep saying that.

Silence.

CLAIRE: I was sitting in a shopping centre the other day. Just sitting, sipping my bubble tea. There were so many people around. I looked down at my tea, and then I looked up again, and everyone looked... They looked the same, but I had this knowledge. I had this absolute certainty that all these *people*... that they were really just apes that had spent a bit too long in the water, lost their hair and put on some clothes. And it was all *wrong*. They weren't supposed to be wearing clothes. They weren't supposed to be talking. They were supposed to go back to being naked and playing in the water and hunting buffalo. It was surreal.

STEVE: Were you okay?

CLAIRE: Yeah, after a few minutes. I told my mind to shut up and ignore it. Just made the rest of the day a bit more disconcerting.

STEVE: When you look at me, do you see an ape?

CLAIRE: *(smiling)* Yeah, a little.

Silence.

STEVE: I still don't really get why you hate them.

CLAIRE: *(sighs)* I don't hate them, Steve.

STEVE: I mean, I get terrified that people will leave. Are you going to leave? If you don't like people, why should you stay? What else is there here? You're kind of irrelevant in the world. If other people aren't important, why continue? I worry about you, Claire.

CLAIRE: I'm not going anywhere. I don't completely agree with you, but I'm not about to off myself or anything. I promise. Okay? I promise.

- **SCENE SIXTEEN**

AUGUST sits in front of John's video camera.

AUGUST: When I was six, a fairy came out of the fairy shop and told me I was special. I've believed her ever since.

Silence.

God, alright, John. You want me to talk about life. Life is... beautiful and terrifying and exciting and hazardous. Life is in the sunrise, the moonbeams, in every piece of grass and every atom of air and drop of water. That's what I hold on to when I forget where I am. That's what keeps me going.

Life's not fantastic. It's not easy. Sometimes it's really damn hard. That's why I try to make it just that little bit better for everyone I meet. No one should pass through my life without being a little better. Leave everything a bit better than you found it.

And I've been doing that, so no one can say it's impossible. I work a job I love and I make a difference. I've had issues and I've seen someone about them. I've still got stuff to figure out, but I'm doing well.

Silence.

The fairy was really pretty. She walked right past my daddy and right up to me, and bopped me on the nose. I realised I had the magic. I was special. Everyone has the magic, but I was special for realising I had it. Does that make sense?

And that means life is fantastic! Until I sit down and think about for a while, and I wonder why I'm trying to make the world better in the first place. Isn't this all temporary? And then I start to get too existential and a little depressive and my head hurts.

But the fairy was pretty.

- **SCENE SEVENTEEN**

GEORGIA and VALERIE having coffee.

VALERIE: So, remind me what degree you're doing again?

GEORGIA: Oh, I'm not really studying. I'm working.

VALERIE: I thought you were at uni a little while ago, though.

GEORGIA: I was. I'm taking a break.

VALERIE: What were you studying?

GEORGIA: Oh. Ummm... Arts/Law.

VALERIE: So you want to be a lawyer?

GEORGIA: No... That's just what I was supposed to want at the end of year 12.

VALERIE: And now?

GEORGIA: I don't know. I think it's hard, with all of these choices. Most kids have no idea where they're going. And the ones that do... well, that often changes. We're basically just floating out there in the ether until we latch onto a solid job.

VALERIE: Mmmm... Yes, well, freedom... *(beat)* It's two years today that I broke up with Brendan.

GEORGIA: I'm sorry to hear that. *(beat)* You're better without him.

VALERIE: But who am I better *with*, Georgia? I don't want to settle. Maybe we're too spoiled for choice. Maybe I'll never be happy. That's a horrible thought, isn't it? That I'll never meet anyone good enough because the right guy is always just around the corner.

GEORGIA: That's the same thing for everything. Jobs, friends, whatever... We choose them anyway. I think we can still judge quality amongst the quantity. Our choice doesn't have to be perfect. Just decent.

VALERIE: Decent. Right.

GEORGIA: I have a job interview next week.

VALERIE: Good luck.

GEORGIA: Good luck yourself.

- **SCENE EIGHTEEN**

CHRIS, FI and JOHN have dinner.

FI: How's the filming going, John?

JOHN: Wonderful, thank you. I'm over half done.

FI: How lovely! Congratulations on the project. Isn't that wonderful, Chris?

CHRIS: I think everyone thinks too much.

FI: Well, I suppose that's one way of looking at it. He doesn't mean to be grouchy, John.

JOHN: I'm used to it. Don't worry. Doesn't bother me.

CHRIS: The lot of you get too sensitive.

JOHN: I don't think so. Besides, you do have a point. I think we do think too much.

CHRIS: You brought the video camera.

JOHN: If we think too much, we may as well record it. So everyone else knows that everyone's thinking too much, too.

JOHN winks at FI, who giggles at him.

CHRIS: Don't do that. Don't wink.

JOHN: I'm allowed to wink.

CHRIS: Not at my wife.

JOHN: Fine. I won't wink.

CHRIS: So you agree: everyone should stop thinking and just get on with their lives?

JOHN: I think we'd be happier. But is that what we want? Is it better to be ignorant and happy than cluey and... potentially not?

CHRIS: When it comes to wanky philosophy? The answer is yes.

JOHN: Are you happy, Chris?

- **SCENE NINETEEN**

CLAIRE sits in front of John's video camera.

CLAIRE: Of course I've thought about killing myself. Hasn't everyone at some stage, with whatever degree of seriousosity. That's a word. I took a Mental Health First

Aid course a while ago, because I find this stuff interesting and I try and collect as much knowledge as possible. And they say, if someone tells you they want to kill themselves, you're supposed to ask them how.

I always thought that was a bit stupid. I've had a couple of friends who were asked that. They thought it was stupid. I asked myself that, and all it did was help me wrack my brains for ways to off myself. On the other hand, it did tell me that I wasn't anywhere near ready to go through with it. I mean, I'd have to do a lot more research on the pills and most of the other methods are too gross for my liking. Too cliché. Too whatever. The pills would be easiest. I've always figured they'd kill me at one stage, anyway. I don't do drugs. I'm talking about meds.

Anyway, that seems to be the point of the question. If they can't tell you, they're not going to kill themselves anytime soon. If they can tell you, then you've got a serious problem on your hands.

So I'm not a serious problem yet.

Please don't question me any more about this when you see this. I really can't stand that. It's not anyone's business unless I say it is, because it's my life and I can do whatever I like with it.

Steve talks to me about people. And yeah, I've done the reading. It's like apoptosis. Pop, pop, pop. Cells in an organism die off when they're not needed any more. Humans do the same thing. Humans kill themselves when they're useless to the population. Pop, pop, pop. Heh. Pop. Population apoptosis. Onomatopoeia. Cute.

Am I useless to the population? I don't know. It'd probably help if I cared about the population more.

Oh. That's the point, isn't it? Once we stop caring, we're useless, so we kill ourselves off.

Cute.

- **SCENE TWENTY**

MAX is getting dressed. JOHN enters, pointing the camera at him.

JOHN: Do you think, Max?

MAX: Do you think, John?

JOHN: I'm serious. Do you think about stuff?

MAX: What sort of shit question is that?

JOHN: I mean, the stuff you left on the camera. You seem to have a lot of strong opinions. But you just... drink and sleep and sleep around all the time.

MAX: Yeah!

JOHN: And most people would be surprised that someone like that... thinks.

MAX: John.

JOHN: Max.

MAX: Why do you think I do all those things?

JOHN: You're living it up?

MAX: Yes. Yes, I definitely am. And part of living it up is not thinking.

JOHN: But you obviously do.

MAX: *(posh accent)* Some people are surprised that I am, in actuality, exceeding intelligent. *(haughty laughter)* And that in actuality, I think all the time. Except when I do the drinking and the sleeping and the hot, hot sex, at which time I am not thinking and that is a wonderful thing about all those things. Okay, Johnny boy?

JOHN: And you'd recommend this approach?

MAX: Highly.

JOHN: So it's better not to think?

MAX: What would you rather? Depressing philosophy, or sex?

JOHN: Touché.

- **SCENE TWENTY-ONE**

STEVE sits in front of John's video camera.

STEVE: It's almost Valentine's Day. She's not going to see this before then, so I guess I can say it. I love Claire. I love her. I don't know a lot of things for certain, but I know that. I've known that for a long time. I guess I've built my life around it.

I don't understand people making themselves islands. Recently, there's just been this influx... That only the individual matters. All we care about are new cars and shopping and this striving for our personal best. That doesn't bother me, but it does bother me when it's the focus point for our entire society. Everyone trying to one-up each other and win whatever they've decided they need to 'self-actualise.'

Silence.

People look at me like I'm crazy. Because I see how we're all connected. That we all matter just as much as each other because we only function as a society. There's a lot of crap being thrown around. People forget each other.

I don't know if Claire knows how I feel. This is a huge deal, telling her. I kind of don't want to. It's not because I'm afraid of her rejection, but because... she's been what's creating personal meaning in my life. We can have personal meaning as well as a collective group loyalty. Claire's mine.

And if, for some reason, I lose Claire, then I lose that meaning.

And my meaning's always going to be a person. I can't help that. People can create their own, put it other places. Mine's... the unbreakable cord I have to the person I love.

And it's almost Valentine's Day. I've been planning this for weeks. I'm going to make her laugh.

I haven't seen her laugh in ages. But you know what they say: when faced with an impossible task, act as if you can't fail. I've got two plane tickets for a month from now. I'm going to give one to her.

And if I'm super lucky, I won't have wasted my money.

- **SCENE TWENTY-TWO**

GEORGIA and CHRIS in Chris's office. CHRIS looks over Georgia's CV. He writes sparse notes as they talk.

CHRIS: You seem awfully young to be so qualified.

GEORGIA: Well, I've always put work first. I'm driven, I work hard, I don't stay in dead end jobs and I suspended my uni degree for real life experience. I'm talking about jobs, I didn't travel or anything. I'm not sure if I'll go back, but in the meantime I hope I'm sufficiently qualified, yes sir. I want to work. That's what I'm good at.

CHRIS: You're not going to leave us in six months?

GEORGIA: Oh, no, not at all. I mean, if I did continue my degree I'd do it part-time by distance or online or something. It wouldn't interfere with my work. And I'd probably only do that if you—as my employer, if you were my employer—wanted me to do that. I mean, this is such a great role. I wouldn't be looking for anything else. I didn't take any leave at my last job except for the mandatory time over Christmas. I could imagine myself here for a long time.

CHRIS: And what about working is so satisfying to you? When are you excited to come to work every day?

GEORGIA: Oh, um, what *isn't* satisfying? Um, I just really want to feel like I'm doing a good job, I guess. I usually know if I'm doing a good job. If I'm hitting my KPIs and if a company is pleased with me. It's always nice to feel as though your work is appreciated. That you're successful at what you do. And I like challenges and learning new things and ticking things off to-do lists.

CHRIS snorts in approval.

CHRIS: Fine. If you're going to be working here you should know that we don't have Christmas closures outside of public holidays. We'll put your formal KPIs together after a month. And I don't like to repeat myself, so listen carefully.

He stands. A second later, she stands, too. They shake hands.

GEORGIA: Are you offering me the job, sir?

CHRIS: I don't repeat myself, Georgia.

- **SCENE TWENTY-THREE**

MAX passes by DAWN, who is reading outside.

MAX: Hello, Dawn. You're looking lovely today as always.

DAWN: Hello, Max. Aren't you a bundle of trouble?

MAX: Never to you, Dawn.

Silence.

MAX: Hey, what do you like to do?

DAWN: Do? I like to do a lot of things, most of which I'm sure you'd have no interest in. Why?

MAX: I mean, what do you do for fun?

DAWN: *(obstructive)* I have a wonderful husband and two children. I couldn't ask for a better church to worship in. All of those things are fun.

MAX: Apart from that.

DAWN: Apart from that?

MAX: Yeah! Like, on your days off.

Silence.

MAX: Oh, come on! There's gotta be something!

DAWN: *(beat)* I collect rare Golden Age mystery novels. I read Wonder Woman comics. I design 50s style skirts and sell them on eBay, with pockets. I make a mean lemon meringue pie. I go bushwalking. I play the piano.

MAX looks very satisfied with himself.

DAWN: What?

MAX: The piano!

DAWN: Is there something wrong with the piano?

MAX: No, nothing wrong with the piano. The piano is perfect. Just like you.

DAWN: Oh. *(beat)* Thank you.

MAX: Any time. Play me something sometime.

- **SCENE TWENTY-FOUR**

JOHN is fixing up his video equipment. GEORGIA enters.

GEORGIA: I've been watching you run around for the last few weeks with that camera, and you know what I realised? That directing embargo you enforced? Is totally off.

JOHN: This isn't directing, Georgia. If setting up a camera in someone's face is directing, we need to re-title all the cameramen.

GEORGIA: You're doing a little more than that.

JOHN: No, I'm really not.

GEORGIA: You're telling people where to sit, and stand, and what to talk about. That's directing.

JOHN: I'm deliberately not directing. Embargo, remember?

GEORGIA: I remember. You never told me why that embargo existed, though. And it seems pretty silly to me. I mean, you're really getting places! Half the people I know are dead jealous of you. I don't know why you'd stop now. *(beat)* I'm just thankful you're still doing *something*, even if it is just playing around with your hand-held like the old days.

JOHN: I'm just... I'm feeling a bit disillusioned about media at the moment.

GEORGIA: Media?

JOHN: Films, books, plays, music... All sorts.

GEORGIA: The first time I saw your room, John... Everywhere there should have been family photos was something from a film. So... What... What could have possibly happened to make you... I don't understand.

JOHN: I just need a break from lies, Georgia.

GEORGIA: From lies?

JOHN: Yes.

GEORGIA: Lies!

JOHN: Yes!

GEORGIA: Because previously, you thought all the films were true?

JOHN: No, not at all. But... they creep into you. I've started expecting my life to function like a movie. I can look at a series of events that happen to me, and say, "There's the inciting incident, there's the midpoint, oh, look, there's the plot point that's supposed to happen on page 90, the climax should be about now and then we'll have the resolution and I'm home free."

GEORGIA: *(beat)* Does it work?

JOHN: Well, I don't really know. Because you don't know how long the movie is. Maybe you've been wrong about the midpoint. Maybe you've just started act three instead of getting past the climax. Was that really the 'darkest point,' or was it just another bump along the way? And you're not really going to live happily ever after, Georgia, you're not. Your movie's not even going to end. Because it's not a movie! It's not a movie.

Silence.

Sorry. I know I'm being a pain in the arse. Thing is, it's not even like I'm being particularly dramatic. I keep expecting... something. You get so caught up in the story that you expect, you actually expect life to be as dramatic as the movies. But it's so washed out. It's like jumping from a children's cartoon into a black and white film about watching paint dry. It just hit me, when I put up the directing embargo. Life's this huge fucking understatement.

GEORGIA: It's not always an understatement...

JOHN: It is, by definition, the boring parts of the story that they take out of film scripts. The brushing the teeth parts. And the things, the things that make sense in music and stories and whatever else—they never make sense in real life. They're lies, but they're harmless, people say. They're little white lies. Well, they're not. Not always. And recently, they've been little black lies, and I've been trying to avoid them. Because no amount of playing the hero, and not giving up, and working hard, and trying, trying, whatever—nothing is going to make any difference any more in real life and when I watch movies or turn on the radio they trick me into thinking I can.

Silence.

GEORGIA: So you're trying to make something that's real?

JOHN: That's the idea. Something where people feel things and think things and nothing necessarily happens. Because that's life. Nothing usually happens. Nothing at all.

- **SCENE TWENTY-FIVE**

Darkness.

STEVE: *(yelling)* Claire! *(beat)* Claire!

CLAIRE: I'm not deaf.

STEVE: Claire. Look, John showed me what you said on the tape.

CLAIRE: Oh, God. Steve... Please. Just leave me alone.

STEVE: No! That's exactly what you said was a problem. You don't want people to connect with you, but you think a lack of connection leads to people killing themselves! So I'm not going to leave you alone any more.

Silence.

CLAIRE: I don't feel well, Steve. Please.

STEVE: Claire. You're not irrelevant. You don't have to have a job, or go to school, or go to uni, or join a club, or join a church, or see your family, or be responsible for saving the world... You don't need any of those things to have meaning. You mean the world to me just sitting there, about to float off into the stratosphere. But please don't float off. Because I love you, Claire. And I'll try and hold you down even if nothing else is.

He flicks on a cigarette lighter. CLAIRE stares at him in the firelight.

STEVE: You're brilliant, you know that? You know so much about everything. Work with John on the video? You'd be fantastic. It's worth it. The stuff you said about balloons and bubbles and birds. Share it with everyone. Say you'll do it? Claire? Will you?

CLAIRE: *(beat)* Okay.

STEVE: Awesome! Thank you, Claire. It'll be fantastic. You'll see.

CLAIRE: You're in love with me?

STEVE: Is that awful?

CLAIRE: No, it's... It's funny.

CLAIRE laughs for some time.

STEVE: *(simultaneously thrilled & heartbroken)* You laughed. You really laughed. Because of me.

- **SCENE TWENTY-SIX**

Dawn's church. DAWN plays the piano. VALERIE enters.

VALERIE: Is there a cat that hangs around here?

DAWN: Not that I know of. We don't have any vermin problems, so I don't see much point keeping one.

VALERIE: Because there's one out the back. There has been the last couple of times I've been here.

DAWN: I haven't seen it. Shoo it away.

VALERIE: I've kind of been feeding it.

DAWN: I'm sorry?

VALERIE: It looked hungry. It's been thinner every time, and it's a nice little cat. We bonded. It's soft, it likes being scratched behind the / ears.

DAWN: Oh. Well, it can't stay here.

VALERIE: I'm thinking of taking it home with me. *(beat)* Would that be wrong? Kidnapping a cat? I'd look after it well, it's obviously not in a good state right now. Whoever its owners are haven't been taking care of it properly.

DAWN: You're not kidnapping it if it's stray. You're getting it off church property.

VALERIE: That's what I think.

DAWN: Are you going to get the cat right now?

VALERIE: Well. Is that okay? I'm days ahead of schedule for the exhibition.

DAWN: Yes, go and save your cat.

VALERIE: I'm calling it Thomas.

- **SCENE TWENTY-SEVEN**

AUGUST and MAX lie in bed.

MAX: Is it over yet?

AUGUST: The clock just ticked over. You have to admit, that was a pretty good Valentine's Day.

MAX: As Valentine's Days go.

AUGUST: I'm glad I know you, Max.

MAX: I should hope so.

AUGUST: And I'm glad I can stop you thinking for a while.

MAX: He showed you the— Ugh! Fucking John...

AUGUST: You know I'm always going to be here if you need me. And you can talk to me if you like. I'm good at thinking.

MAX: Yeah...

AUGUST: I liked what you said.

MAX: Yeah?

AUGUST: I wouldn't be sleeping with you if I didn't think you were smart. And interesting. I think we have something good.

MAX: Yeah, I think so, too.

AUGUST: I'm going to call my family, okay? I haven't talked to them in ages and they're getting antsy.

MAX: It's midnight, August.

AUGUST: Not in their time zones.

She grabs her phone and dials.

- **SCENE TWENTY-EIGHT**

JOHN is playing back footage on the video camera's internal screen. He's showing GEORGIA. The footage stops. JOHN shuts off the camera.

JOHN: So, what do you think?

GEORGIA: *(genuine)* I really like it.

JOHN: Good. I made it for you.

GEORGIA: For me?!

JOHN: Yep.

GEORGIA: You're not in love with me, are you?

JOHN: No!

GEORGIA: Good! You scared me for a minute there. Why on earth did you make this for me?!

JOHN: It was mostly that first night. You just seemed so down, you know? I wanted to show you... most people are lonely. Everyone's searching for something or has already put in safeguards for... securing their tethers. It's not just you.

GEORGIA: I knew that already, John.

JOHN: Then it's a pleasant reminder.

JOHN packs up his video camera.

GEORGIA: It's all very postmodern.

JOHN: What does that mean?

GEORGIA: Don't worry. *(beat)* Thanks for keeping me company.

JOHN: Thanks for the idea in the first place.

JOHN holds out his hand. GEORGIA takes it.

GEORGIA: Hey, John?

JOHN: Yes?

GEORGIA: It's Sunday night.

END

HOW TO DIRECT FROM INSIDE

CHARACTERS (in order of appearance):

BLUE/EVE: A young woman. As Blue, she includes:
    NATASHA: Domestic Blue.
    ALEX: Blue at work.
    SARAH: Teenage Blue.
    MAGGIE: Actress Blue.
    BRIONY: Blue as a student.
SUSIE: Blue's memory.
JACQUELINE: Blue's imagination.
ILLIA: The director.
KAT: A heart sprite.
ANNE: A heart sprite.

SETTING:

Inside of Blue's body. Melbourne, Australia. The present.

A NOTE ON FORMATTING:

A forward slash (/) is used to indicate when the next character begins speaking before the first character has finished their line(s). Wherever a forward slash appears inside a character's dialogue, the next character should begin to say their line(s) immediately. This will lead to two characters speaking at the same time for at least a moment; this is wholly intentional and is mandatory for all productions.

- **SCENE ONE**

BLUE (early 20s) cautiously slips through the curtains onto the stage. More than a dozen pockets are sewn to both the inside and the outside of her coat. Most of these pockets are full, although we cannot see their contents.

She addresses the audience.

BLUE: Oh... You were expecting me.

I can't actually see any of you. Lights are too bright. But I'll assume you're there.

I guess I can entertain you.

BLUE glances around the stage and into the wings, searching for other actors. She finds none.

BLUE: I have a confession to make. I don't like monologues. There's not much you can say in a monologue that you can't portray in a dialogue, or otherwise show on stage without exposition, exposition, exposition.

But it would be... impractical... to explain this with other people on stage, so I guess I'll keep going.

So, I looked at my wallet a minute ago, and apparently my name is Maggie. Actually, my wallet said Margaret, but I'm making an executive decision that it's Maggie.

She rifles though the coat pockets.

I have a lot of wallets in here. One for Alex, one for Briony, one for Natasha... I kind of lost count of how many. The coat's pretty heavy, and it just seems to get heavier...

There's one thing that everyone agrees on, and that's the woman in red. She links us all together. Of course, she doesn't always wear red, at least not in real life... But real life never impacted on us that much.

She's always in red in my dreams. Whenever I remember my dreams, I dream about her. She has a name, of course, but she's so entirely whole to me that it wouldn't be right to define her in any one box.

I don't have a name in the dreams. I don't need one. And I know I'm wearing blue without even looking down.

(fiddles with pockets) I keep flashcards in here. Each one is a dream I've written down, because they all form part of this elaborate story that hasn't finished yet.

At the moment, it starts off when we're celebrating Red's birthday at Disneyland. It's 1.15 am and I'm about to head home when someone hands me a glass of champagne. I sip through about half of it when I realise that "shit, it'll take my liver another hour 'til I'm sober and able to drive" and the next thing I know—because there's a big gap in the dreams here that's yet to be filled—we're both standing in the middle of the desert in some military facility under the burning sun, and Red collapses on the sand engulfed in fever.

The rest of the plot makes more linear sense. It has some nice moments, too, where we finally make it back to the city and she's so happy, she actually lifts me into the air. Or where we escape from these poisoned factories, and we run to meet each other amongst crowds of chaos under these halogen streetlights... And she looks like she's aged about ten years since I last saw her... Her skin has this frightening translucent quality about it... But I smile, because there's nothing better than seeing her, and reach my hand up through the night air to brush her cheek, and tell her she's just as beautiful as ever.

We used to have this theory, the lot of us, that cultivating a crush in the right place was really useful. There are few better motivations to perform well.

Maggie met her a few years ago when she was selling temporary passports. The only price was your passion and your focus, and she'd been in the business a long time. Bet she could make you a thousand pockets if you shadowed her. I had a few, but not enough. Not even enough to hide a few packets of Panadol.

Meeting her was electric.

She took Maggie's whole life, really.

I didn't mean it to. Alex says you nurture a crush like a seed, choosing the right place for it to grow and exposing it to sun gradually, and watering it so it grows towards the light and can absorb all the richness the sun has to offer. It's a business plan. It's an investment in engagement and concentration.

It was only a problem when Red had a similar plan. "You can't underestimate the power of tension, Maggie. That's what really makes the sale."

By the time I realised I'd lost control of the game she'd gotten Alex with ambitious new corporate goals and practically murdered Briony in her book-covered sleep and Natasha... Well, after Natasha's last break-up she had Natasha with a single smile.

It's a trick up your sleeves, I guess. When you're in the identity business.

Alex can't fault her. Not one bit, because the seed did grow to something worthwhile. Her heart's more like a suit jacket at this stage, but we all sacrifice something, don't we?

But I could never leave. You need the temporary passports to combat all the pockets she's sewn, pockets you've filled. You need to be able to shrug off the coat you wove for yourself.

I'm light in my dreams. I'm light when I'm simply Blue.

The lights fade down. BLUE prepares to leave the stage, then catches sight of the audience. She stares.

BLUE: You're wearing black today.

Snap to black.

- **SCENE TWO**

BLUE lights a candle and carries it upstairs to Susie's attic. The door creaks from lack of use. SUSIE (11), a pretty, pale little girl stands by the windows, partially illuminated by moonlight.

SUSIE: I don't know why you bother.

BLUE: Do I frequently disappoint you? We don't usually converse.

SUSIE: No. *(pause)* If it wasn't for Briony I wouldn't get any visitors at all.

BLUE: Well, you don't have anything to scare Briony about. You're healthy, aren't you?

Silence.

SUSIE: Am I really that scary? I can't tell you anything new. Anything old you've survived at least once. I can't see why it would bother you so much.

BLUE: Doesn't mean you want to relive it again.

SUSIE: If you relive it enough, it'll stop bothering you.

BLUE: I'd rather not be completely desensitised to everything at this point.

BLUE sets down the candle. She picks up a moth-eaten doll from a pile of old-fashioned toys in the corner.

BLUE: Why do you keep these?

SUSIE: Where else should I put them?

BLUE: You could toss them out.

SUSIE: There's only a few left. The attic used to be filled with dolls, before you brought up that acid. Then I had to throw them out, didn't I?

SUSIE reclaims the doll from BLUE and resets it into its original position.

SUSIE: You need to keep a few, Natasha. You'll get lost without them.

BLUE: I'm perfectly fine. Alison or Sarah might have lost something important, but not me.

SUSIE: Alison's buried in the backyard. Sarah's not dead. She's sleeping in the corner behind the dolls, actually.

BLUE: What?

SUSIE: You want everything wrapped in these neat little packages. Something or someone happens, but they don't happen any more, so you want to throw them away. It doesn't work like that!

We all have this terror that if we stop announcing our existence for one second, we're going to stop existing. But you take that to the extreme; if it's not around right now, it was never around. And I have to sit in here trying to protect you from burning everything.

BLUE: Like everything in here is so precious!

SUSIE: It is!

BLUE: But if it's in here, it's not important any more! Just old and painful.

SUSIE: But it is important, because without it, you wouldn't exist.

BLUE: Burning these isn't going to affect me!

Silence.

SUSIE: So you are going to burn them.

BLUE: I didn't say that.

SUSIE: What's the candle for, then?

BLUE: So I don't trip on the stairs.

SUSIE: Don't be silly.

Silence.

SUSIE: You burn them, the whole place is going down.

BLUE: Maybe.

SUSIE: Sarah, too?

BLUE: Will she wake up?

SUSIE: No. She hasn't woken in months. You could wake her.

BLUE: *(she considers this)* No. Survival of the fittest.

Silence.

SUSIE: What about me?

BLUE: Well, I need you.

SUSIE: You need me. Why?

BLUE: Don't be stupid.

SUSIE: No, I want to hear it from you. Why do you need me?

BLUE: Because otherwise, everything falls apart!

SUSIE: So you should listen to me when I tell you not to do something! Shouldn't you?!

BLUE: *Yes*! But that wasn't me!

SUSIE: I watched you do it.

BLUE: I mean, I wasn't myself.

SUSIE: You were as Natasha as ever. You were practically born that day.

BLUE: But I didn't do it on purpose! *(pause)* It just happened, okay. I'm sorry. I'm sorry I wasn't strong enough to realise what I was doing. I'm sorry. I just wanted to forget about the pain for a while.

SUSIE: But you can never get them back.

BLUE: I know.

SUSIE: Pity.

BLUE: Is it?

SUSIE: It is to me.

Silence.

SUSIE: So why come back this time? Didn't learn any better?

BLUE: Might as well finish what I started.

SUSIE: Ten years later?

BLUE: Long enough that nothing in here matters any more.

SUSIE: Just because they're not a part of you doesn't mean they're worthless. They're a part of me.

BLUE: I've never been a big fan of you.

SUSIE: Yes, I know that.

Silence.

BLUE: You think I should've made peace by now?

SUSIE: I think you're smart enough to go down those stairs without leaving an inferno behind you.

BLUE: I think that's a funny way to measure intelligence.

SUSIE: I think you're far more illogical than I give you credit for.

BLUE: Well, you're fucking up here playing with dolls!

SUSIE: Arranging them.

BLUE: What?

SUSIE: Arranging dolls.

BLUE: For fuck's sake...

Silence.

SUSIE: Just go. Pretend that this never existed at all, if you like. I don't care. Ignore it and it might as well be gone. You don't have to search and destroy everything that makes you the slightest bit uncomfortable. You can just leave here and never come back. *(pause)* If you're that cowardly.

BLUE: Fuck you, Susie. You have no idea what it's like.

SUSIE: No, I don't.

BLUE: It's not a question of bravery.

SUSIE: Isn't it? We destroy the things that scare us. It's all throughout history.

BLUE: History doesn't interest me.

SUSIE: That's part of the problem.

Silence.

SUSIE: Are you going to leave now?

BLUE: I haven't decided yet.

SUSIE: You know I'm right. *(pause)* I'm going to blow out the candle now.

BLUE: Don't.

SUSIE: Why not?

BLUE: Give me a reason to keep this.

SUSIE: Because if it all went up in smoke, why wouldn't the exact same dolls come back the next time? Who's to say Sarah wouldn't come back? And if you don't want to repeat her, then don't give yourself a chance to forget why she was a mistake in the first place.

BLUE: She wasn't a mistake. She's just not relevant any more.

SUSIE: Didn't you hear what I just said? *(pause)* Do you really want to have to relearn everything that brought you here? Haven't you been through enough? Once should be enough.

BLUE walks towards the door and puts her hand on the doorknob.

SUSIE: I'm going to blow out the candle now.

Silence. Simultaneously, BLUE opens the door and SUSIE blows out the candle.

- **SCENE THREE**

JACQUELINE leads a blindfolded BLUE.

BLUE: We're in the city... for whatever reason. It's a cold night. I'm only in a shirt and skirt, because I've left my suit jacket and tights back in the office, and I've left my heels in her car. I'm tip-toeing along the concrete... I spot a building across the street, grab the cuff of her shirt and tug her towards it. All the cars have stopped. I announce...

JACQ: Come on, I have a surprise for you.

BLUE: And she just raises an eyebrow sceptically as she follows me towards the lift.

I take her to the thirty-fifth floor. I don't say anything, but that's okay. The elevator doors open, and everywhere there's luxury and chandeliers and this wide, open dome roof floors above us to the night sky. And she says...

JACQ: You're taking me to dinner—again?

BLUE: *(laughs)* No. Anyone can do that.

And I take her *(laughs)* to the ladies' toilets *(laughs)* on level 35. And she says...

JACQ: I don't need to pee, Alex.

BLUE: Neither do I.

Because on one side of the ladies' bathroom on level 35 is an entirely glass wall, overlooking the city as far as the eye can see. An ocean of glittering lights, blinking and spinning all the way to the horizon. The Ferris wheel, the stadium, the ships sailing across the harbour...

And we stand there, side by side, silently staring at the city. I can see her smile reflected in the glass. She really likes it.

JACQ: Gee, that's aiming low.

BLUE: Fine, she loves it.

JACQ: Better.

BLUE: And I pull out a bottle of wine and two glasses from my bag, and grin, because I know no one else has ever taken her on a date like this. Because none of them would've been allowed in the ladies' toilets on level—

BLUE's face falls dramatically.

Shit! Shit, where's my fucking report. 62B, sub-clause seven. Thank God.

BLUE tears off her blindfold and the lights fall.

- **SCENE FOUR**

ILLIA lights a cigarette.

ILLIA: I woke up this morning, and I felt like I hadn't slept at all. My eyes were burning in my head, and I realised that I didn't know how many tickets we sold last night. I barely remembered what the show was like. So I'm like, fuck, we have to do something here, people. Can't go on like this or we're gonna lose the plot altogether.

Seems to me our whole life has been one big-arse production and performance week, simultaneously, and you've got to be fucking crazy to do that just for one week, you know? That's fucked up. And yet here I am, and we're still doing it ten years later. I'm exhausted. More of you keep popping up backstage—great, we appeal to a larger audience—but the budget can't handle it and sometimes I don't even know who to send out on stage any more.

I mean, you get situations where people who know Alex and Natasha are in the same room, and you can't send them out at the same time. So you either get this panicked tag-team thing, or you can't send either out without fucking something up, so you end up with an empty stage. And boy, that's shit. No one wants to buy tickets to an empty stage.

And I'm sitting up here, with my grandé coffee and my notebook, and I'm trying, trying to put on a show... Because that's all I really want to do, you know? That and catch some shut-eye once in a blue moon.

So I guess I'm just gonna say it. I need to cull someone. Some of you get a stack of applause, but the rest of you are pretty poor. Love you guys, I do, you're very useful or you wouldn't exist in the first place, but perhaps you're more suited to crew right now. Or maybe we should just get rid of you altogether. Frankly, the production's going pretty bloody brilliant, but we need to keep it fresh and snappy; we need to trim the fat if we're going to keep it a success.

I don't have the time to conduct this process, really. I have to sit here and manage the lot of you 24 hours, seven days a week.

So you've got five minutes to convince me not to kill you off.

(she points to an audience member) Go.

- **SCENE FIVE**

BLUE opens a panel of the box JACQUELINE is hiding in.

BLUE: Don't.

JACQ: Don't what?

BLUE: I didn't want to see you again.

JACQ: You're seeing me now.

BLUE: I've clocked off work now.

JACQ: Then what's the problem?

BLUE composes herself.

BLUE: I was in a meeting.

JACQ: Okay.

BLUE: So get out of the box.

JACQ: I like the box.

BLUE: Get out of the box, Jacqueline.

JACQ: Do you not appreciate the lovely pun?

BLUE: I was in a meeting!

JACQ: Did it not go well?

BLUE: Well, I missed half of it!

JACQ: Okay.

BLUE: I missed it because of you.

JACQ: Do you not like me? *(pause)* Then why do you visit me?

BLUE: Because... you're very...

JACQUELINE pops out of the box and kisses BLUE.

JACQ: Attractive?

BLUE: Distracting.

JACQ: Fabulous.

BLUE: No, not fabulous. Bad. Horrible, awful. I hate distractions. I am here to do my job. You don't factor into that.

JACQ: But I do.

BLUE: Don't you remember our last conversation?

JACQ: *(sighs)* You asked me to leave.

BLUE: Yes, I did. Very tactfully and politely, if memory serves.

JACQ: Sure.

BLUE: And you haven't left.

JACQ: No.

BLUE:	You are infuriating!
JACQ:	Well, it was a stupid request.
BLUE:	I am trying to do my job. I am trying to do my job. What part of that don't you understand?
JACQ:	And if you remember correctly, I had my dissent noted on the putting of that motion, on the grounds that it was a knee-jerk reaction that we had not discussed enough.
BLUE:	And the motion was carried anyway.
JACQ:	It shouldn't have been. The chair can't vote, and we're a committee of two.
BLUE:	This is not a committee! You will listen to me, and you will leave me alone.
JACQ:	I was.
BLUE:	And when I come and visit you, you will send me back.
JACQ:	You only missed the boring bits.
BLUE:	Those bits are the ones I actually need to listen to.
JACQ:	Then have a bit of self-control.

Silence.

BLUE:	Do you realise how difficult it was to say goodbye to you? You're the best part of my day. But... I need to do this.
JACQ:	Why?
BLUE:	Because if I'm not good at my work, then I'm nothing.
JACQ:	Without me, you'll be pretty crap at your work.
BLUE:	My efficiency will skyrocket.
JACQ:	Will it? Is that all your care about?

BLUE: I suppose so.

JACQ: Why are you so desperate to get rid of me? Have I not been good to you? Have you not enjoyed our expeditions?

BLUE: I need to get rid of you... because every time I visit you, it reminds me of where I am. It reminds me that I could be somewhere else, out of the office, doing something... fun. With people I actually want to be around, not that I'm simply forced into friendship with. That I could be comfortable, and relaxed, and happy, and not here.

And if I can't imagine I'm somewhere else, then I can't be disappointed I'm not there.

JACQ: What about... the woman in red?

BLUE: What about her?

JACQ: Well, you don't expect anything to actually happen between you two.

BLUE: No, of course not.

JACQ: Then why bother?

BLUE: Why bother what?

JACQ: Loving her.

Silence.

BLUE: I don't understand how this is relevant to—

JACQ: What I mean is, you don't think about things, you don't invest in them just because they're going to eventuate. You can enjoy things and then let them go.

BLUE: Alright. But it's not like those things, those not-being-in-this-office things, are never going to happen.

JACQ: You'll probably always be in some office.

BLUE:	Yes. But maybe someday I'll enjoy it enough that I won't want to leave.
Silence.	
JACQ:	Let me walk you through your day without me. Alright?
	8.30 – You park your car, but you can't imagine how long you're going to be in the office, so you buy a whole-day ticket with the cash you were going to use to buy lunch.
	9.00 – Your office is messy. You feel like you should clean it, but you can't imagine how the office would look like clean, so you don't.
	9.30 – Your boss stops you in the hallway and asks your opinion on the proposed new floor plan. You have no opinion, because you can't possibly imagine anything but this.
	10.00 – The photocopier breaks down. You can't imagine what went wrong with it, so you don't try to fix it.
	10.30 – You're in a meeting. Finance wants a larger desk. You have no idea what the consequences would be of said larger desk, so you're utterly useless.
	Shall I continue?
BLUE:	Alright! Alright, alright, enough. I get the picture.
JACQ:	So you understand now why I couldn't possibly leave you?
BLUE:	Yes. I understand.
JACQ:	Just because you remember me best for my escapist purposes, doesn't mean that's all I'm good for.
BLUE:	Okay. I'm sorry. I hadn't taken that into account.
JACQ:	One of your greatest talents is the ability to think outside the box. Now, I don't have to get back in there, do I?

BLUE: No. I appreciate you a lot more now.

JACQUELINE grins and kisses BLUE.

JACQ: I'm very glad to hear that, Madame Alex. Now, you have a bit of a window before your train leaves, is that correct?

BLUE: That's correct.

JACQUELINE ties a blindfold around BLUE's eyes.

JACQ: Where shall we go? The beach?

BLUE: No, I'm tired of the beach.

JACQ: Skydiving? Water skiing? Commanding your own army?

BLUE: The park, I think.

JACQ: The park? Just the park? Isn't that a bit boring?

BLUE: Not when you're there, Jacq.

JACQUELINE grins and pulls BLUE offstage.

- **SCENE SIX**

ILLIA in her office, pausing only for occasional moments of stillness and juggling multiple cigarettes:

ILLIA: Dear Girls,

I don't think you understand. You have all these problems with the schedule, the schedule, but you're up in arms about one of you disappearing from the cast. You can't have it both ways. There's either a bunch of you and you have to fight for space, or there's a few of you who get to have a relaxing time because you rule the roost. There is no third option. You only have one body to occupy. And besides, you're the ones who've chosen to do it like this. You didn't have to make this situation where it's so fucking crowded backstage you can barely breathe.

Let's have a bit of communication here. I'm the schedule bitch, but I can't work miracles. We can only be in one place at one time.

It's been particularly bad lately, I know. And partly that's because there's more of you and partly I don't know why. Maybe you can tell me. Because I'd love to make it simpler for us, I would. Yes, I can live without you, but so can you, to be entirely honest.

To answer your question, Briony, I will not replace Alex so that you can make your exam. Exams do not sell tickets. Exams do not earn applause. All they give us is a bad hair day and a little less sanity backstage, and I think we all agree we need to save that up at the moment. So I hardly see you! I don't give a shit. There's a reason why you're not around much, and that's a good enough reason for you to be pretty much at the top of my cutting list. Please stop bothering me. I won't be answering any more correspondence relating to this issue.

One of you please fit in a hairdressing appointment somewhere, this thing is getting out of hand.

Warm regards, blah, blah, blah...

  Illia

- **SCENE SEVEN**

ANNE and KAT slump over each end of a motionless seesaw. The steady trickle of liquid can be heard close by.

BLUE enters with a splash, clutching a map.

KAT: Hey, Sarah.

BLUE: Hello. How'd you know it was me?

ANNE: Who else would it / be?

KAT: It's nice to meet you.

ANNE: *(warning)* Kat.

KAT: Anne. *(to Blue)* Excuse us. We're very tired today.

BLUE: No worries. Why so tired?

ANNE: Why do you think? We've / been busy keeping you alive.

KAT: Anne!

BLUE: Oh. Of course. Thank you.

KAT: *(sighing)* What brings you here, Sarah? Not that we don't appreciate your company, but there are plenty of nicer places you could be right now.

ANNE: I don't appreciate her company.

KAT: Don't be a shit.

ANNE: I don't! I'm trying to spend my last few minutes in peace, and now I'm forced to make polite conversation?

BLUE: I don't want to interrupt you! This won't take a minute. I was just worried, and I was sent here to clear some things up.

KAT: How can we help?

BLUE: *(beat)* I'm worried I don't have a lot of time left.

KAT: In what way?

BLUE: I'm worried I'm dying.

ANNE laughs.

BLUE: I'm glad that's so funny for you. I thought you'd be able to at least tell me something helpful.

KAT: Please excuse Anne, Sarah. She gets stressed sometimes.

ANNE: Sometimes!

KAT: Well, / you do!

ANNE: That's rich.

BLUE: Please! Can't I... Can't you give me an answer?

KAT: No, you're not dying.

Silence.

BLUE: So everything here's working properly? It's just a coincidence that I've been so out of it for the last few months?

KAT: Well...

ANNE: Can't you tell the liquid's rising?

KAT sighs.

ANNE: She has a right to know.

BLUE: It's not usually like this?

ANNE: It doesn't usually rise, because we pump it out. The blood comes in, we pump it out and around the body. That's the way the system works.

BLUE: But you're not pumping.

ANNE: No.

BLUE: Why aren't you pumping?

KAT: We got old. We've been doing this for 12 years.

BLUE: Twelve years!

KAT: We're tired.

BLUE: Why? Why are you tired already? I'm young. I don't want to die!

KAT: Twelve years is the maximum. No one should live past that. / You expire.

BLUE: Don't be stupid! Get up! Why are you doing this to me? *(pause)* Please don't kill me because you're too lazy to keep me alive!

ANNE: It wouldn't make any difference.

BLUE: Why?!

ANNE: Because we already stopped. The blood is rising. It's too late to pump it out. In a few minutes, it'll be high enough to drown us anyway.

BLUE: You're drowning yourselves?

KAT: It'll be a relief.

ANNE: And in a few minutes, we'll be born again and have to pump again for another fucking 12 years. But at least we won't be exhausted any more.

BLUE collapses on the ground in front of the seesaw and sits leaning against it.

BLUE: Why 12 years? Doesn't everyone have longer than that? Twelve years is nothing!

ANNE: If you haven't already evolved into someone else in 12 years, you're damn well due to.

BLUE: So I'm dying because I'm out-of-date?

ANNE: You're not dying, sweetheart. You're dead. / You died several minutes ago.

BLUE: What?!

KAT: *(to Anne)* Did you have to do that?

BLUE: I'm not dead yet! I'd know if I was dead!

ANNE: No, you wouldn't.

KAT: Little-known fact of the brain: it keeps firing for 12 minutes after the heart stops.

Pause.

ANNE: I think I did her a favour. You can't really be alive until you know what being dead's like. Nothing exists without the opposite to compare it to.

BLUE: What does that even mean?

ANNE: There's no good without evil. You can't tell if something's hot if you haven't experienced cold before... You can't know what it's like to be alive unless you've been dead. For the couple of minutes before your brain stops completely, you finally have something to compare it to. You can finally appreciate it.

KAT: That's a very bleak view.

ANNE: But it's true. It makes logical sense. We take everything for granted unless we have a worse alternative.

KAT: Also a very dangerous view.

ANNE: I think the world began... and no one lacked anything, so nothing existed. And then suddenly, someone realised that something was missing, that they wanted something... and then it snapped into being, because a lack of it existed.

KAT: Why don't you take your own advice, Anne, and be quiet so the three of us can enjoy the last moments before we expire?

ANNE: Excuse me for letting the girl fully appreciate them.

KAT: She could've done that much better if you hadn't told her she was dead.

ANNE: I don't think so.

KAT: Well, she looks pretty miserable now, doesn't she?

BLUE: Stop talking about me as though I'm not here.

KAT: *(beat)* I'm sorry, Sarah. You don't have to stay here. You should go somewhere nice.

Silence.

BLUE: How much longer do I have?

KAT: I'm not sure. About three minutes, maybe.

BLUE: Where will you guys go?

KAT: I don't know. That's the exciting part, I guess. The not knowing.

BLUE: Why do you do it?

KAT: Do what?

BLUE: Pump in the first place?

ANNE: You wake up, you're on a seesaw, there's an instinct to jump. When you stop the blood rises and you drown. It's not that hard to figure out.

BLUE: I guess not.

KAT: You got any unfinished business?

BLUE: Doesn't everyone? No one ever tells everyone how they feel, or does everything they want to do before they die. You have to expect to be disappointed.

KAT: Wherever we're going, she's going to do a lot of stuff that you can't do. We can pass on a message from you. If you like.

BLUE: Yeah, okay... Tell her... that she can be whoever she wants to be. That however you act like tends to be how

	you turn out. That it's usually worth telling someone that you love them, even if you don't expect anything back.
KAT:	This person you love... Were you with them now?
BLUE:	Well, I was, actually. For a short time. Before I died. Didn't know I'd never see them again, did I?
ANNE:	We'll tell her.
BLUE:	You remember this stuff? This stuff from before you drown every time?
KAT:	Not really. But we have our ways.
ANNE:	Your message will get through.
BLUE:	Yeah?
ANNE:	Yeah.
BLUE:	I'm glad you told me this was the end.
ANNE:	Good. I can tell you next time, if I see you again.
BLUE:	Good. *(pause)* It'll be better next time, right? I'll be better next time.
KAT:	Yeah. Yeah, you will.
BLUE:	Next time, she'll know I love her.

- **SCENE EIGHT**

The start of this scene is a perfect echo of scene one:

BLUE:	But I could never leave. You need the temporary passports to combat all the pockets she's sewn, pockets you've filled. You need to be able to shrug off the coat you wove for yourself.

I'm light in my dreams. I'm light when I'm simply Blue.

The lights fade down. BLUE prepares to leave the stage, then catches sight of the audience. She stares.

BLUE: You're wearing black today.

The moment hangs in the air for a couple of seconds. ILLIA walks onto the stage, takes BLUE's arm and leads her off.

ILLIA: That was very interesting! Excellent work. I don't know quite what to make of it... I'm not used to you directing yourself. But good, very good. And the audience loved it. I was going to wait until tomorrow night to pay you, but what the hell...

ILLIA starts counting out a pile of money in five cent coins.

BLUE: Illia...

ILLIA: Mmmm?

BLUE: I have a problem.

ILLIA: What, you too? If it's about a new wardrobe, I'm sorry, it'll have to wait. I really need to buy Alex a pair of new shoes. People in the office are going to start laughing at her.

BLUE: No, it's not about that.

ILLIA: Yes?

BLUE: Well, you saw what happened out there?

ILLIA: I saw you give a great performance.

BLUE: I mean at the end.

ILLIA: Well, you didn't know quite when to get off the stage, but that's okay, honey. You haven't done that bit before.

BLUE: No. I mean, she *knows*.

ILLIA: Knows what?

BLUE: How I feel.

ILLIA: Well, that's a bit of a shock, but you'll get over it.

BLUE: But I'm not shocked. I'm not nauseated. I'm not mortified. I'm nothing.

ILLIA: So that's great!

BLUE: It's not great! Don't you understand? She finally knows, and I don't feel anything any more. There's no reason to see her. There's no reason to do anything. I've finally done it and there's nothing left.

ILLIA stops counting the money and finally gives BLUE her full attention.

ILLIA: What are you saying?

BLUE: I'm saying... I don't know what I'm saying yet. I don't know what to do with myself. What do I do if my life doesn't revolve around her? I don't know! Isn't that hilarious? I don't / know!

ILLIA: She broke your heart?

BLUE: No, she didn't do anything. It was fine. Everything was fine. Everything is a nice, tidy little book and now it's over and done with but I have to keep going.

Maybe.

Briony wants to talk to you.

ILLIA: For fuck's sake.

Alright, fine, bloody hell. Put her on.

BLUE transforms into Briony.

BLUE: You haven't been returning my messages.

ILLIA: That's right.

BLUE: Why not?

ILLIA: It's your responsibility to slot yourself into the schedule. First in, best dressed.

BLUE: I do slot myself in. Then you give priority to the others, and they all book themselves in over me.

ILLIA considers this for a moment.

ILLIA: That's very true.

BLUE: Why?!

ILLIA: Two reasons. One, you're unpopular with the masses. I even wanted to follow Natasha's storyline for a while back there. At the moment she's a bit boring but we're seeing who we can pair her up with in the future. I'm thinking movie star, someone in the film industry. It'd be good for Maggie.

Second reason. You're piss weak. Problem is, the others are all fucking passionate over whoever this Red woman is; they're all really motivated and they generally do a really good job. You don't have that. I don't even know if you want to be here. So you get bumped down.

BLUE: I do want to be here! Would I be arguing with you now if I didn't want to be here?

ILLIA: I don't know. Do you like to argue?

BLUE: The thing is, I could sell your tickets. I'm smart. I'm charismatic. I do a good job—

ILLIA: Not lately.

BLUE: Not lately because I've hardly gotten any time at all! You throw me, what, three measly hours a week? What the hell is that? How am I supposed to rehearse and perform with that? I don't even get a tech run any more. You say

	I'm doing badly but please, what do you expect? You have to give me something to work with!
ILLIA:	I'm not giving you any more because there isn't any more time to spare.

Silence.

BLUE:	Maggie says I can have her slots.

Silence.

ILLIA:	What?
BLUE:	Maggie says I can have her slots.
ILLIA:	No. She's not leaving. No, no, no, no.
BLUE:	She's taking a break.
ILLIA:	No one takes a fucking break! She cannot quit on me. No. This cannot happen!
BLUE:	Illia!
ILLIA:	You tell her that she is being a bitch about this. You tell her that she can have a couple of days off to get her shit together and then she is right back on the stage. Hear me? You hear me, Maggie? Better yet, get her out here. Get her out here right now.
BLUE:	Illia...
ILLIA:	I said now!
BLUE:	She's already gone!

Silence.

BLUE:	I'm sorry.
	Look, she might come back.

ILLIA: Yeah, I don't know about that.

Silence.

BLUE: You know, that's why you should keep me. Because I don't depend on the applause of the crowd. I don't depend on anyone else. It's just me. The outside world isn't going to affect me at all.

ILLIA: So you're like this strange, exotic hermit creature that's somehow immune to the virus, huh?

BLUE: Yeah.

ILLIA: You want a cigarette?

BLUE: No thanks. You know what those do to you?

ILLIA: Don't care to.

BLUE: I do.

- **SCENE NINE**

BLUE puts on some music and curls up in the corner of ILLIA's office.

ILLIA enters, carrying a pile of reports.

ILLIA: Alex? I'm free now. Do you wanna get a coffee?

BLUE: I'm not really in the mood, to be honest.

ILLIA: For coffee? Seriously? It's only one o'clock. You're always in the mood for coffee.

BLUE: My stomach's not co-operating.

ILLIA: That sucks.

Okay, well, I have about 10 minutes before I'm gonna get desperate for caffeine. We can talk here. What's up?

Silence.

BLUE: I'm kinda freaking out, Illia.

ILLIA: Why's that?

BLUE: It's just the last few days... I feel like I've been doing everything all wrong. My stress rash came up again, and there's just not enough time. There's never enough time.

ILLIA: Maybe we should get you something to drink...

BLUE: No, I don't want anything.

ILLIA: I have a really nice white under my desk.

BLUE: Alcohol is not a good answer for me.

ILLIA: Fine. Fair enough.

Look, a lot of this place has gone to shit recently, but the shit's temporary, just like everything. How we get by now is how we get by any other time. By performing. We pretend everything's fine and act exactly as normal, and no one knows anything's wrong, so everything keeps working perfectly. And then by the time things pan out again, the rest of our lives haven't gone to shit as well.

BLUE: So I just keep pretending everything's okay?

ILLIA: Absolutely. For now, at least.

BLUE: I'd kind of forgotten that.

ILLIA: Does that... give you something to deal with it for the moment?

BLUE: Yeah. Yeah, I feel a lot better, actually.

IILIA: Good. Because now I have a couple of questions for you. I've been getting all these reports of my cast trying to dismiss my crew. You know anything about that?

BLUE: Probably.

ILLIA: The crew are there for a reason, and the show can't go on without them. Do you understand me?

BLUE: Absolutely.

ILLIA: Good. I would really like this company to grow to a stage where we're not fighting all the time. That's not productive. That gets all of us into shit and wastes our time. Can you pass on that message for me, Alex?

BLUE: Sure.

ILLIA: Fabulous. Was there anything else you wanted to discuss with me?

BLUE: No. Thank you.

ILLIA: Shall we go and get a coffee?

BLUE nods.

ILLIA: Excellent. Thank you, thank you, thank you.

- **SCENE TEN**

SUSIE: Things to take to an exam: three pencils, HB; two pens, blue; one eraser; one water bottle, label removed; one calculator, no cover. Turn off your mobile phone and place it in your bag under your desk.

BLUE enters, picks up her bag and walks past SUSIE, kissing her on the cheek.

SUSIE: Good luck.

BLUE: What would I do without you?

They smile warmly. BLUE exits.

ILLIA enters. She sips a cup of coffee and attempts to hand one awkwardly to SUSIE.

ILLIA: Here.

SUSIE: I thought you didn't want to know me.

ILLIA: That's not true. I just get busy.

SUSIE: You're not busy now?

ILLIA: I made time. *(pause)* Take the damn coffee, will you?

ILLIA shoves it into SUSIE's hands. SUSIE takes it this time.

SUSIE: What's wrong?

ILLIA: Surely you know.

SUSIE: Of course I know.

ILLIA: So you don't have any comments?

SUSIE: Aren't you the director?

ILLIA: Very cute.

SUSIE: Aren't you?

ILLIA: I don't always have the answers. The cast isn't a machine. They have emotions, unfortunately.

SUSIE: And here... You're looking for answers?

ILLIA: What I want to know... is what kept them going before Red? What got them excited? What motivated them before they met her? Because then we can get that back.

SUSIE: Do you really need to look that up?

ILLIA: Why do we even have a record keeper?

SUSIE: It's just kind of obvious.

A dangerous pause.

ILLIA: Surprise me.

SUSIE: It's the same reason they need a director, Illia. It's the same reason you have such a big cast. If they didn't care about it, there'd only be one of them. There'd be no reason for more.

ILLIA: So what is the reason?

SUSIE: Approval.

ILLIA: *(beat)* Approval?

SUSIE: Of course. You could have a one-woman show, but you send out different versions of the same woman to gain approval from different people.

ILLIA: Yes. Or we wouldn't sell any tickets.

SUSIE: That's the theory.

ILLIA: We wouldn't! We wouldn't please anyone. We'd go completely under.

SUSIE: How do you know that?

ILLIA: Because I remember my mistakes, back when I sent out the wrong ones, and everything went to shit.

SUSIE: That was a long time ago.

ILLIA: Not nearly.

SUSIE: Well, I gave you your answer.

ILLIA: No, you said 'approval.' That's not a solution.

SUSIE: Sure it is. You can take it one of two ways—

ILLIA: Yes?

SUSIE:	Yes. You can find someone new to transfer that approval onto—
ILLIA:	Like me?

Silence.

SUSIE:	No. They don't much like you, actually.
ILLIA:	But they respect me, don't they? Thus they want my approval.
SUSIE:	No. They fear you. They have to win your approval, otherwise you kill them. That's not the sort of motivation you're looking for.

Silence.

ILLIA:	Then who..?
SUSIE:	I don't know. There isn't anyone.
ILLIA:	There isn't anyone? In all of these books? In all of those dolls? There's no one they want to impress?
SUSIE:	No.
ILLIA:	You're kidding me.
SUSIE:	I do not tend to joke around.
ILLIA:	Yeah... Fucking fair enough.

Silence.

SUSIE:	The second option?
ILLIA:	Yes?

Offstage, ANNE screams shrilly. ILLIA flinches in shock and spills her hot coffee onto SUSIE, who screams as well.

ILLIA:	Fuck! I'm so sorry. I gotta take this... Be okay! Please!

ILLIA rushes off.

- **SCENE ELEVEN**

ANNE and KAT (now young again) stand mid-pump on the seesaw. They stare, horrified, at BLUE, who stands in the middle of the room holding a gas can and a lit candle.

JAQUELINE rushes in; stops abruptly when she sees BLUE. Moments later, ILLIA does the same.

ILLIA:	What the hell?!
JACQ:	Why'd you stop pumping?
BLUE:	I told them to stop, or the whole place goes up in / flames.
ANNE:	Please... If you're hesitating, then you don't really want to do this. Let us keep going.
BLUE:	Don't you dare.
ANNE:	You have the gas already! You don't need two methods of killing / everyone!
BLUE:	Maybe I do.
ILLIA:	For God's sake!
JACQ:	Maggie... / Please...
ILLIA:	Stop this madness! Maggie, what are you doing? You're ruining everything—
BLUE:	No. I already did that. There's nothing left here. Not just for me; for everyone.
JACQ:	That's not true!

BLUE:	Be quiet! I was just going to torch the attic, but then I remembered what Susie told Natasha about repeating her mistakes. And there's no point in doing this over.
KAT:	It was supposed to be a favour!
JACQ:	What?
KAT:	Telling her! It was what you wanted... Sort of.
ILLIA:	Blow out the candle.
BLUE:	No.
ILLIA:	Do it!
BLUE:	No!
JACQ:	Be quiet, Illia!
ANNE:	Can we please just start pumping?
BLUE:	Shut up! Everyone shut up!

Silence.

KAT:	Why are you doing this?
BLUE:	I don't want to just survive.
JACQ:	Let's go the beach, Maggie.
BLUE:	I don't want a fucking Band-Aid!
JACQ:	That's—
ILLIA:	Isn't there anyone you care about?
BLUE:	No. Not enough.
ILLIA:	Then just give me a minute, and we can work this out.
ANNE:	We don't have a minute, Illia.

JACQ: There are other options.

KAT: If you loved her so much, where did that go?

BLUE: I'm going to light it!

Silence. JACQUELINE whispers something complicated in ILLIA's ear. It involves a lot of animated hand gestures and throws BLUE off guard.

Once JAQUELINE is done, ILLIA pulls a cigarette out of her pocket and lights it.

ANNE: The hell are you doing?

ILLIA gives the cigarette to JACQUELINE, who walks casually towards BLUE, cigarette between her teeth, and gestures for the gas can. BLUE, curious, hands it over. JACQUELINE transports the gas can a few 'safe' paces away.

JACQ: Do you want me to light this?

BLUE: Not really.

JACQ: Why not?

BLUE: Because I want to do it.

JACQ: Really?

BLUE: Yes.

ILLIA: What if I didn't care about the tickets any more?

BLUE: You only care about the tickets.

ILLIA: What if I didn't? What if I cared about you?

BLUE: Why would you care about me?

ILLIA: Because you're important to me.

BLUE: For ticket sales.

ILLIA: For other things.

BLUE: Really?

ILLIA: Really.

BLUE: If I'm not bringing in the tickets, why would you keep me around? Why not just use the others?

ILLIA: Maybe I wouldn't be selling tickets.

BLUE: Then we wouldn't make any money.

ILLIA: Maybe we don't want money.

BLUE: Don't be stupid.

ILLIA: Maybe we don't.

BLUE: Then we wouldn't have a show.

ILLIA: Exactly.

BLUE: What 'exactly'?

ILLIA: Then you wouldn't care about impressing anyone.

BLUE: Okay.

ILLIA: So it wouldn't make any difference whether you had to perform for her or not.

BLUE: Maybe.

ILLIA: Maybe you could just be happy.

BLUE: I don't know if that would work...

ILLIA: Blow out the candle. I'll prove it to you.

BLUE: You promise?

ILLIA: I promise.

BLUE blows out the candle.

JACQUELINE hands ILLIA the cigarette, which she accepts gratefully.

ILLIA: Thanks.

JACQ: Any time. You realise in my version, you don't exist any more.

ILLIA: I gathered that.

- **SCENE TWELVE**

ILLIA is at her desk, doing paperwork. She hears BLUE enter.

ILLIA: Don't tell me you're a fucking 'nother one.

BLUE: Another one?

ILLIA: Sorry, bad week, blah, blah, blah... What's your name, where should I fit you in the show? Sell your case to me. Time is limited so you better be good. How she keeps coming up with all of you, I'll never know.

BLUE: Eve.

ILLIA: Welcome to the crazy, Eve. Strap yourself in. Where shall I place you?

BLUE: There's not really anywhere to place me. I'm everyone. I'm the whole show.

ILLIA: What?

BLUE: So it won't be so crazy any more.

ILLIA: The bastards up and left? In the 10 minutes I've been doing paperwork? I thought they were asleep! You've got to be joking!

BLUE: They didn't up and leave. We just couldn't handle contradicting ourselves any more. It was too hard. Performing is one thing, but without something to unite us... all of the split parts couldn't function on our own.

ILLIA: That's why they needed a director.

BLUE: You have to concede that wasn't working as well as you'd hoped.

ILLIA: *(beat)* Maybe.

BLUE: I'm just all of them in one.

ILLIA: Do you need a director?

BLUE: Only sometimes.

ILLIA: That's probably for the best.

Silence.

BLUE: I don't want to always be putting on a show. Sometimes it's important to just... be. You know?

ILLIA: That sounds attractive.

BLUE: You can try it now, if you like.

ILLIA: Aren't you going to work soon?

BLUE: In a little bit, sure.

ILLIA: Isn't that a performance?

BLUE: It doesn't need to be.

ILLIA: No?

BLUE: No.

ILLIA: This confuses me.

BLUE: That's okay. I guess we realised it's more important to have a healthy cast than a successful show.

ILLIA looks concerned by this suggestion.

BLUE: Maybe Jacqueline can take you to the beach. You ever been there?

ILLIA: Is there coffee?

BLUE: There's whatever you want.

ILLIA: Well... alright then. Tell me how it goes.

BLUE: I will do.

ILLIA starts to exit, then pauses.

ILLIA: Eve...

BLUE: Yes?

ILLIA: Did you end up finding what you were looking for?

BLUE: Yes.

ILLIA: *(beat)* I'm glad.

Silence.

BLUE: Goodnight.

ILLIA exits.

BLUE shrugs off the coat she's been wearing for the entire play. Underneath she is wearing light blue. She ruffles her hair and adjusts her clothes so that they're more comfortable.

Around her, the other actresses start to clean and re-set the space, as if the play is over and they are completing their post-show jobs.

After a few moments, Blue joins in. When they have finished their jobs and re-set the space, everyone exits.

END

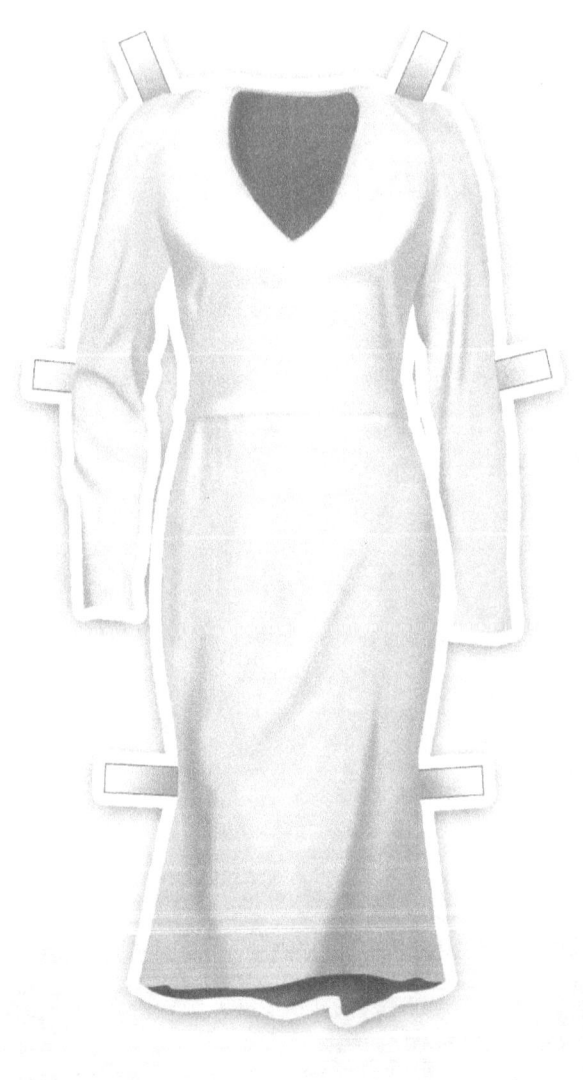

MATCH GIRLS

CHARACTERS (in order of appearance):

THE WITCH: Of silver hands and candy houses.
THE QUEEN: Of talking mirrors and poisoned apples.
THE PRINCESS: Of bright and burning light.

SETTING:

Not our world. Not our time.

A NOTE ON FORMATTING:

A forward slash (/) is used to indicate when the next character begins speaking before the first character has finished their line(s). Wherever a forward slash appears inside a character's dialogue, the next character should begin to say their line(s) immediately. This will lead to two characters speaking at the same time for at least a moment; this is wholly intentional and is mandatory for all productions.

Darkness. Three women sit behind three candles. From left to right, they are:

THE WITCH (19), *in a long-sleeved black dress, both her hands dipped in silver paint.*

THE QUEEN (30s), *in a long-sleeved crimson dress. Blood has run down from her forearms and dried in drips along her hands. A blindfold is tied around her eyes, but must not impair her vision completely.*

THE PRINCESS (17), *in a long-sleeved white dress. Her hands and lips are also white.*

WITCH: One fine day behind the mill, / my father chopped off my hands.

QUEEN: The queen's first child was a small, strange-shaped boy with / a tumultuous spirit.

PRINCESS: *(lights a match)* The queen died shortly after childbirth, of internal burns. The baby princess lay crying in the corner. They knew this because of the wails; the baby was so bright that they could barely see her limbs, let alone her features. By some curious genetic match, or perhaps mutation, instead of the slight glow of her countrymen, the princess radiated light. The king could not hold her for more than three seconds without burning, and besides, looking at her hurt like staring into the sun. *(blows out the match)*

QUEEN: *(lights a match)* The queen's first child was a small, strange-shaped boy with a tumultuous spirit. When he was three, he developed an eye infection and went half-blind, and then when he was seven, by accident or design—she could never decide which—he poked out her eyes with a two-pronged fork. *(blows out the match)*

WITCH: *(lights a match)* One fine day behind the mill, my father chopped off my hands.

He did it with an axe, on a tree stump. He said the devil was coming. That he had promised the devil my hands, in exchange for his life. *(blows out the match)*

I did not believe in the devil. My father had been hearing voices for some time.

There was a lot of blood, but no pain. I had heard stories of soldiers, those with their arms sliced off who screamed, not because it hurt but because of the shock of seeing their shoulder and limb separated. The pain is so great that your body snuffs it out.

I yelled, too. I shrieked. I clutched my bloody wrists to my dress and backed away, sprinting, stumbling into the forest. My father did not pursue me; the devil could find me anywhere, if I were still wanted.

I curled up at the base of a tree, nesting in its roots. The pain arrived like a delayed traveller. I thought, *I am going to die.*

QUEEN: *(lights a match)* The queen ordered her huntsman to steal the boy and abandon him deep in the forest. The king would throw him in the dungeon or to the firing squad, and she assured herself the forest was a kinder alternative. When her huntsman returned with the bleeding heart of a stag, the queen announced it as her son's; *(blows out the match)* he was now as dead as she was blind.

While the pain in the queen's face gradually lessened, the king scoured the land for something to ease the pain in her heart. At the other edge of the forest he came across a weathered cottage belonging to an old man. For a small fortune, the old man sold the king three items: a mirror, a white-gold knife and a vial of clear liquid that bubbled perpetually beneath its cork.

The king and queen hung the mirror beside their bed. It was enchanted to describe whatever it reflected, so that it could function as the queen's replacement eyes whenever the king could not. Then the queen took the knife and the vial into the snow, knelt in her thickest dress, and prayed for a child the exact opposite of her first: a girl, pure and breathtakingly beautiful as the snow beneath her gloves.

PRINCESS: *(lights a match)* As the princess grew up, the king scoured the land for potential suitors. On her sixteenth birthday he brought her the Ice Prince. His icy body reflected her light and, although she was better adjusted than others to her own radiance, this almost blinded her. She clamped her eyes closed over the starbursts in her eyelids and held his hand through his thick glove. Seven seconds later he had to pull away; his palm was melting into the glove's fingers. *(blows out the match)*

QUEEN: *(lights a match)* As per the old man's instructions, the queen drank the contents of the vial in one gulp, and soon after dozens of her veins protruded as thick blue ridges. She felt for the ridges on the exposed skin of her arms, cut seven different veins with the enchanted knife and let the blood fall onto the snow. She had not expected to feel so lightheaded. *(blows out the match)*

When she woke in the snow minutes later, she was pregnant with her second child.

WITCH: *(lights a match)* I did not die. I woke with my wrists attached to my dress, the brown of dried blood mixing with the brown of the fabric. They stuck, knitting with the cotton where I'd pressed them tightly to stem the blood flow. *(blows out the match)*

My wrists were swollen, ballooning, fiery things. With effort, I pushed myself up the tree trunk by my feet, and the bark scraped sharp against my back.

I began to walk.

It was a long walk. Several seasons changed. My wrists healed, turning into knots of scar like the knots on an old tree. I took pleasure in small, animalistic activities: biting into a sun-warmed peach and letting the juice run down my chin, diving to the bottom of a river and propelling myself up with jack-knifed legs.

In spring, blood appeared between my legs and again, I think, *I will die.*

I did not die.

Later, it came again, many times.

I didn't die then, either.

In the heart of the second autumn, I stumbled through a pile of leaves into a clearing. Low, golden sunshine illuminated the charred ruins of a house. And within the ruins, something glinted, metallic and inviting.

I stepped gingerly over the rubble and peered at my treasure. Nestled safely and impossibly intact: a pair of silver hands.

I dropped to my knees.

With infinite care, I wiped each hand along my tattered brown dress until the dirt disappeared. The joints in the fingers swung back and forth, more or less like a real hand. There was no rust, no squeaking. When I slipped the metal cuffs of the hands onto my wrists, they fitted exactly, as if they had been made especially for me.

PRINCESS: *(lights a match)* On her seventeenth birthday the king brought her the Water Prince. He left slightly wet footprints on the tiles of her room. He was naked aside from a pair of damp shorts, and tiny water droplets constantly beaded on top of his skin. He took her in his arms and neither melted nor burnt. She was light as air as she savoured the feeling of his skin, his muscles under her palms, his lips on her neck.

Twelve seconds later he pushed her away. *(blows out the match)*

He said she was boiling him on the inside.

QUEEN: *(lights a match)* Most days, the queen cradled Snow White to her chest and had the mirror describe every detail of her daughter's tiny frame. Afterwards, glowing with pride, the queen would ask, "Who is the most beautiful in all the land?" And the mirror would coo:

WITCH: "You,"

QUEEN: ...directly to Snow White and add:

WITCH: "She grows more beautiful by the day."

QUEEN: *(blows out the match)* For years the queen's heart swelled fat with happiness. Her daughter's tinkling laughter filled every hallway in the palace. And then Snow White's seventh birthday arrived, and her screams echoed down the hallways instead.

The adults found three dead bodies in the parlour: one beneath the window, one face-down in the birthday cake and one impaled on the spinning wheel. When the doctor later questioned Snow White, he had barely laid eyes upon her when he collapsed, knocked his head on her bedpost and promptly died.

PRINCESS: The king declared that there were no other suitable men in the world. Even he, himself could not marry her. She would never bear children. He locked her in a tower at the edge of the ocean, believing the only thing she was useful for was becoming a lighthouse. *(lights her candle)*

During the night, she slept, a ball of light illuminating the rocks below. During the day, she cooked with the heat of her hands and the supplies in the basement, and she examined the world map on the wall. A corner in the south-east had been torn off. It seemed deliberate, like a jilted lover tearing a face from a painting.

WITCH: I had avoided people, for the most part, since my hands were stolen. Now I felt buoyed, lighter. I jogged to the nearest town, contented simply by the burbles of conversation, the currents of humans flowing past each other in the shopping district.

So many man-made shapes and colours made my head spin. I wandered past shops selling thick, salty-looking ink in glass flasks; glazed hams suspended from ceilings; doorways with silk jackets encrusted with precious stones.

QUEEN: "You!"

WITCH:	A booming masculine voice hit me in the ear, not three paces away. I stopped, glanced around. He was looking directly at me.
QUEEN:	"Are you going to pay for that?"
WITCH:	My heart hammered in my chest. I looked down, and saw a large bag of flour and a smaller bag of brown sugar clutched in a silver hand. I was a criminal. I was mortified. I felt about to faint.

The other silver hand curled, reached into my pocket and pulled out three gold coins. I stared. I had never had any money of my own, and this did not feel like mine, either.

The merchant huffed and held out his own sweaty hand.

"I'm sorry," I whispered in my rusty voice, dropping the coins down into his palm. He nodded like he didn't believe me.

I took off along the cobblestones, down the streets into the forest. The silver hands did not feel like my hands any more. I could not move the fingers of my own free will, and yet they had moved. They had curled and grasped and extended without my consent.

I shook, pressing one hand between my knees, pulling back my arm to wrench the hand away like an unwanted glove. I grunted. But no matter how hard I pressed or pulled, the hand always stayed a part of me.

I tried again with the other hand to no avail. |
| QUEEN: | The princess was inconsolable. She opened her door only to her mother, who brought her the sweetest of apples and braided the whitest of ribbons in her hair. And as the hours rolled on and the queen braided and braided, a hot, dark knot grew inside the queen's stomach and made her gasp. |
| PRINCESS: | Sometimes she stood at the gigantic tower window and wished she could jump. She thought she could probably |

	reach the waves, but she'd never learnt to swim; the glare in the water had always been too bright.
WITCH:	When my tears fell, I let them fall on the silver, and I wished fervently that it would rust.
QUEEN:	When she could stand it no longer, the queen brought Snow White before her magic mirror and asked, "Mirror, mirror, is my daughter breathtakingly beautiful?" And the mirror said:
WITCH:	"Yes, of course,"
QUEEN:	...and added:
WITCH:	"She grows more beautiful by the day."
PRINCESS:	During the day, she dug a hole in the bottom of the tower, shoveling dirt with a silver spoon.
	At dawn on her eighteenth birthday, the Light Princess escaped and rushed south-east. She took only the spoon, a knife, and as much food as she could carry. At sunset, she hid in caves or buried herself in the ground, with just enough space for her eyes, nose and mouth. And before too long, blissfully, she crossed the border into the next kingdom.
WITCH:	I took the flour and sugar to the clearing, to the ruins of the house. I remembered a formation of low bricks, sticking out amongst the wreckage, which gave me the impression of an oven.
	I searched through the rubble for any other bricks, stacking them together, interlocking them with the remnants of the old oven. The silver hands grabbed everything easily, nimbly, more skilled at construction than I ever was with my own flesh. They fitted the oven together like an expert puzzle.
PRINCESS:	Many things in the Metal Kingdom hurt her eyes, including the Metal Prince. She could only sit on the prince's lap for twelve seconds before heating him so much that he burnt her flesh, and she ended up falling

backwards and almost cracking her head open. The burns took three weeks to heal. She wondered why everything she didn't burn on first contact turned painful.

After that she came to either the Earth Kingdom or the Steam Kingdom. If it were the Earth Kingdom, its ochre-coloured prince glared from under his dusty eyelashes and forbade her from coming any closer. He believed his arteries were stems, his veins were shoots and his capillaries were roots. One touch and his entire circulation system would ignite.

QUEEN: The king would return to the kingdom soon. The queen refused to live without her husband, or without her daughter. She had already lost one child. She would not lose another.

The queen dug deep in the earth and retrieved the enchanted knife from so many years ago. If the princess' face was not so beautiful...

WITCH: I am ashamed to say I went back to the town. More than anything, I felt I was starved of opportunity.

The hands had made me ravenous.

From the stalls they picked jars of cinnamon, towers of sea salt, cloves and ginger in wooden boxes, eggs in woven baskets... And each time, a silver hand dipped into my pocket and fished out gold coins. I never saw the coins fall in, but I learned to recognise the slight weight in my pocket, the tiniest clink as the silver hands pilfered someone's pockets or bags.

I returned to the clearing laden with parcels.

I sat in the rubble and pressed the cinnamon and ginger to my nose, inhaling deeply. I rubbed an exquisite, perfectly smooth egg against my arms, face and neck. I tipped a little of the salt onto my tongue and reveled in it, my eyes sliding shut.

And then the hands really got to work.

QUEEN: Snow White woke to find the knife inches from her nose.

The princess fled, out through her bedroom window and far into the depths of the forest. The huntsman followed. With each of her daughter's steps the queen felt her own veins constrict and her heart grow tight, like a dangerous weight was multiplying on her chest.

The huntsman caught Snow White within the hour. She cried that the queen had tried to kill her; she drenched his jacket with her tears. She said, "Please, don't take me back there, or she'll try again!" And the huntsman, who could only see the faintest glint of her eyes in the darkness of the new moon, killed a boar and took its heart home instead.

The queen did not believe him. Her veins told her the girl was still alive, not eaten by wild animals as the huntsman claimed. But the queen's grief was real and there was no advantage in the truth, so she lied and thanked him for finding the remains of her daughter's body. She would not send others into the forest; it was a suicide mission, for those with eyes.

WITCH: Deep in the woods, though not that deep, stood a house made entirely of gingerbread. The walls and roof and floors were gingerbread, as were the chimney and single iced door. If you licked the windows you would know them to be sugar, and if you bit into the windowsills you would know them to be marzipan.

The house did not age, nor rot, nor melt. Encrusted in the gingerbread were hard candies of every flavour and colour, liquorices which sparkled, candy-covered chocolates in the shapes of hearts and stars and clovers.

Inside the house there lived a woman, though she was only recently a girl. They say idle hands are the devil's work, but how fervently I wished mine would stop.

The silver hands were always moving, like mechanical spiders desperate to get out of the rain. Sometimes they cleaned and scrubbed and tidied. Sometimes they played over my body, prying open my mouth and feeling my tongue, the ridges of my teeth. Sometimes they crawled between my legs and played me like an instrument, running their fingers inside me and warming with my body heat.

Sometimes I didn't mind.

PRINCESS: If it were the Steam Kingdom, she laid her hands on its prince's shoulders while his scalp steamed gently. In seven seconds, wisps of steam began to seep from the rest of him. They rose to scald her on the face and arms and hands. She cried and her tears went up in steam, too.

WITCH: Mostly, they liked to cook. They liked sugar. They liked ever more elaborate desserts, which never seemed to go off and piled in towers, gathering on surfaces and in ever-expanding nooks and crannies. They cooked shelves and cupboards for more cooked treats.

They cooked another room for the house.

Often, at night, I suffocated the hands beneath my mattress and felt them struggle, twisting, beneath my body weight. After a little while they gave up. Alone, unmoving, quiet washed over me. Bliss.

There were usually scars from this ritual when the hands broke free; long scratch marks across my torso, legs or back, one or two or five in a row, but they were always worth it.

And then, one day, a gap in my wall appeared, and on the other side a chewing child.

QUEEN: When he had barely turned eight, the queen's son came across the weathered cottage belonging to the old man.

PRINCESS: "Please,"

QUEEN: ...howled the muddy boy...

PRINCESS: "I'm starving and I can hardly see. Won't you help me?"

QUEEN: And the old man offered him a deal.

From deep in the basement came a pair of enchanted scissors, their blades tinged with crimson, which snipped off seven of the boy's eight fingers. Where the fingers fell on the dusty floor, seven copies of the boy grew slowly to full-size and stood naked, shivering in the evening air. Once they had been dressed in the old man's identical, oversized work shirts, the old man said:

WITCH: "Now you share the hunger and thirst of one boy between the eight of you. Which one is coming with me?"

QUEEN: They drew straws. One of the boys clambered onto a loaded wagon, the old man flicked the horses' reigns, and the remaining seven watched from the porch as an eighth of themselves rolled away.

WITCH: They froze when I opened the door: a boy with his mouth stuffed with gingerbread, and a girl with her lips wrapped around my windowsill. They were short, sickly pale and bony, their wide blue eyes protruding too far out of their skulls. I suspected they were not much younger than I was.

The boy swallowed hastily, the girl detached her lips.

"You must be very hungry," I said.

The girl smiled and dug her fingernails into her other arm.

PRINCESS: "We've walked for three days,"

WITCH: ...she said...

PRINCESS: "with very little food, and are lost in these woods, and our parents can't feed us any more."

WITCH: Eventually, I said, "If you believe you shall starve if you don't come in... you may."

The children's faces relaxed with joy. A silver hand pushed the door fully open, and with barely restrained hunger, they darted inside.

QUEEN: It was dusk, years later, when Snow White stumbled upon the same cottage. She found numerous grimy, makeshift beds, seven bloodstains on the ancient wooden floor, and a trapdoor with the largest silver padlock she'd ever set eyes on. She was in the process of leaving when its occupants appeared silhouetted in the doorway.

The seven boys stepped inside, axes and rabbit corpses over their shoulders and streaks of mud on their chins. They stood only slightly taller than Snow White—their aging was spread between the eight of them—and they stared at the hazy, girl-shaped blur in their living room and started to whistle.

But Snow White cried that the queen had tried to kill her, and there was nothing they could have bonded better over.

PRINCESS: If it were the Earth kingdom, she cut through the curtain of vines across its border with her knife. If it were the Steam Kingdom, she reflected her own light with her silver spoon, and thus shone a pathway through the thick, suffocating clouds of steam to the other side.

WITCH: I fed the children like they'd never eaten in their lives.

I brought them: sticky date puddings drenched in hot fudge; towering chocolate cakes with sparkling shards of caramel, raspberry and mint strewn in three layers; macaroons in 12 different flavours; scones with jams and the fluffiest creams; and melted chocolates.

When they'd eaten their fill, groaning with pleasure on my benches, I made them a bed of marshmallows in the corner of my living room.

I cleaned for some time to delay my own sleep. The hands had been delighted all evening, practically dancing off my wrists, and the guilt ate at me like acid. I knew I should send the children on their way directly after breakfast.

Later, under my blankets, the hands did not want me to rest. They wanted to play.

I decided I wouldn't put them under the mattress that night, wouldn't make them angry with the children in the house.

PRINCESS: Regardless, she reached the south-east corner of the map.

WITCH: I would send the children away in the morning.

QUEEN: The queen needed no manufactured disguise. Her veins pulled her always in the right direction, and the closer she grew to her daughter the easier the pressure on her heart. But she had nothing to navigate the step-by-step terrain, and by the time she emerged at the cottage she looked like she had fallen through the forest horizontally. This bloody, exhausted, filthy woman bore little resemblance to the queen who had first stepped from the palace.

So much so that Snow White spied a beggar through the window, and called out:

PRINCESS: "We have nothing to spare!"

QUEEN: And the queen unbuckled her shoulder bag, explaining she expected to be giving rather than receiving gifts, and held up her offering.

The bodice was truly beautiful, but what really drew Snow White were its shining white ribbons. As the queen laced her up, the girl thought of all the times her mother had adorned her with similar ribbons, and how warm and loved she had felt—before the deaths. The beggar's hands were wonderfully gentle, until they paused, and then the laces pulled tighter and tighter until Snow White was having trouble breathing.

With one hand, the queen held her daughter by the ends of the ribbons. With the other, she pulled the white-gold knife from her boot. And then she heard the low, dangerous whistling of a mob approaching from the hills, so she released the ribbons and fled.

PRINCESS: The palace was made of smooth, black stone that didn't shine. Inside, the king and queen seemed to suck much of the colour and light from the air. It was a peaceful kind of darkness, and they apologised that they had never had a son, and there was no Dark Prince for her to procreate with.

QUEEN: Snow White fell to her knees on the blood-stained floor. The whistling turned into a stampede of small footsteps, and the many versions of her brother clawed at the bodice until she was free.

WITCH: I was still half asleep when a third hand appeared on my shoulder.

PRINCESS: "Are you alright?"

WITCH: ...asked a female voice.

My eyes snapped open. The girl's blonde hair, inches away, was almost iridescent white in such early dawn. Unaccustomed to either company or shame, I threw my arms to either side of me.

PRINCESS: "You were making noises."

WITCH: I tried to control my breathing, tried to restrict the bile rising up my throat. "Noises?" I whispered.

PRINCESS: "Murmurs, mutterings in your sleep... You were having a nightmare?"

WITCH: I considered the girl's open face. A small glob of melted marshmallow was stuck to the side of her forehead.

"Always," I said.

We padded through the front door and around to my back garden: little more than two fruit trees and a small hill of seeded soil. The girl stared at every fruit and every leaf, cataloguing and greedy.

I held out my arms. "You're very welcome."

She fell to her knees before a dozen strawberries, shovelling them into her mouth with dazzling efficiency. I sat nearby, my hands drawing meaningless patterns in the damp dirt. In the end she left three on their stems, wiping the crimson juice from her lips. Her hunger seemed to still.

I suspected it was rude to ask, but the children would be gone in a matter of mouthfuls. "Do you despise your parents, for letting you down?"

PRINCESS: "Why would I despise them? They did their best."

WITCH: "They almost killed you."

PRINCESS: "They sent us away because they couldn't bear to see us starve before their eyes. I can't hate them for that."

WITCH: She picked a fat lemon from the tree and peeled the skin with a combination of fingernails and teeth.

PRINCESS: "We aren't starving any more, thanks to you."

WITCH: She came and sat next to me, too close; my hands might have damaged her. I scooted back. In the dull light I was uncertain, but I thought her face fell.

"It's not personal," I said. "I lost my hands a long time ago."

PRINCESS: "They seem to work well enough."

WITCH: "They're not..." I was afraid, suddenly, that the hands could hear me. "They're not really mine." The last word morphed into a gasp as a sharp silver finger dug into the flesh of my side. A tiny darker patch appeared on my brown dress.

Perhaps the hands could hear; perhaps they simply sensed intention.

The girl was up on her feet. She hesitated for a moment, rocking back on her heels, and then kicked the offending hand away from my side. With her right knee, she pushed my shoulder to the ground and pinned the hand with her left boot. It convulsed like a dying spider.

My other hand was blessedly still.

The wind had been knocked out of me. I lay with my head in the dewy grass, staring up at the frightened girl. Her shin was warm along the side of my torso. I couldn't remember the last time I had touched someone.

PRINCESS: "Do you need bandages?"

WITCH: ...she asked.

PRINCESS: "Something else?"

WITCH: I shook my head against the grass. "I don't think it's deep. It will heal like the others."

PRINCESS: "Others?"

WITCH: The hand stopped its convulsions after one last spasm, but the girl didn't move away.

"There's a town to the east of here," I said. "A bit less than half a day's walk away. You should head there. Take as much food as you want, I insist."

She didn't respond. Instead, she looked over her shoulder at an empty wire cage.

PRINCESS: "Is that for meat?"

WITCH: "Chickens," I confirmed. "But years ago." I was hit with old memories of the hands snapping their necks.

She nodded.

PRINCESS: "Are we safe to go to breakfast?"

WITCH: I took several moments considering the frozen hands. They were play-acting, surely, but I suspected they'd behave until their next calculated moment of rebellion. "If we behave," I said. "Though they shan't like you leaving."

PRINCESS: "I'm not planning to leave,"

WITCH: ...said the girl.

QUEEN: When the queen returned to the cottage the following day, she came brandishing a glittering comb which cast sunspots through the window. The lights danced along the inner walls, mesmerising Snow White and beckoning the girl outside.

The queen apologised for running off during their last encounter. The whistling alarmed her, she said; could she offer this comb as compensation? And Snow White coveted the comb like a magpie and longed for those motherly fingers in her hair, so she swung open the door.

Manipulating her daughter's curls between her fingers, the queen struggled to keep from weeping fat tears down the back of the girl's neck. She wrapped Snow White's locks into a glossy roll and wielded the points of the comb like a weapon.

But the whistling came again, louder this time and instantly chilling. The comb fell to the floor with a raucous clatter, and the queen had vanished by the time it stilled by Snow White's feet.

WITCH: Breakfast passed in relative silence. At one point the boy reached over and scratched the marshmallow off the girl's forehead. She smiled at him and crinkled her nose, and I felt a stab of jealousy for that kind of companionship. That morning, the hands had refused me any liquid but melted chocolate in a mug. I took tiny sips: sickly sweet.

With a couple of short, insistent gestures the girl directed the boy to my back garden. She followed, announcing she'd be back in a minute, and either I believed her or the silver hands did, because they made no move to cease scratching patterns into the sides of my mug.

The girl did return shortly, without her brother but with a strange sort of smile. She tossed a second lemon in the air between alternating palms.

PRINCESS: "We should do it,"

WITCH: ...she said.

PRINCESS: "What you were talking about in your sleep."

WITCH: I felt instantly naked.

PRINCESS: "We should eat the boy,"

WITCH: ...she said.

PRINCESS: "Cook him."

WITCH: The only sound was the lemon thumping in her hands.

She pressed on:

PRINCESS: "I mean, not even chicken for years. You must be starved for meat. I've locked him in the cage." *(beat)* "Go and see."

WITCH: I heard the blood beating in my ears. I stepped outside; the cage had not moved. The boy was curled against the far corner, one blue eye open and fixed on me.

I took another step and he cried out. I was speechless.

QUEEN: "Not any closer!"

WITCH: ...he yelled.

QUEEN: "I know what those hands can do!"

WITCH: I held them up, clear in front of me. The silver fingers wriggled.

QUEEN: "You put them away!"

WITCH: The venom in his voice made my throat constrict. I tucked my hands tight behind my back, which was the best I could do. I ventured another step.

Like a well-practiced magic trick, he revealed a rusty key—the key to the cage—and winked. It disappeared again.

I took out the silver hands.

QUEEN: "Are you going to eat me?"

WITCH: I realised with relief that the hands couldn't reach him while he was caged.

"Not now," I said, to buy some time. "I have to fatten you up first. You're so thin, it would hardly be worth cooking you now."

His tears came right on cue, and when I returned inside to his sister, she was sitting cross-legged on my dining table and squeezing lemon juice onto her tongue.

QUEEN: There was no more time. The queen had advised that she might be absent for several days, but they would have dispatched an official search party by now. So she lingered closer to the cottage than was strictly safe, listened for the sound of the mob departing and crept to the window one final time.

She pulled a perfect, scarlet apple from her bag and set it on the windowsill. With the white-gold knife, she cut a chunk of ripe apple flesh and brought it past her lips. There was no unusual tang or toxic aftertaste. She had expected something bitter, or at least abnormal, given that she'd submerged the entire apple in poison days earlier.

Snow White was smiling as she ate the rest of it; the queen could hear it in her voice.

The queen could not bring herself to smile. She murmured, "You are loved very much," and left her daughter alone to die.

PRINCESS: She slept in a deep, deep basement in the palace and slept for a long, long time.

QUEEN: Several hours later, the queen's horsemen hoisted Her Highness onto a black mare and returned her to the palace. She retrieved the antidote from a hole in the back of her dresser, a thick liquid stoppered in the same vial she'd used to conceive her daughter seven years earlier. Her veins were quieter than they'd been since Snow White's departure, and the antidote caught in her throat.

When her veins relaxed completely, the queen was hunched behind her bedroom window, cradling a length of white ribbon. Her daughter took a last, fevered breath in a nest of bloodstained blankets and expired.

The seven copies of her brother discovered her body in the morning. They locked her in the corner of the basement, inside the thick glass coffin that had been gathering dust there.

PRINCESS: "Do you have an axe?"

WITCH: My hands paused in the middle of kneading lemon-scented cookie dough. "No," I told her, and the hands start up again.

PRINCESS: "How do you chop firewood, then?"

WITCH: "No firewood." I pushed a lock of hair out of my face with my shoulder. "I use oil."

The girl's mouth cracked open.

"It never seems to run out," I confessed, and found I couldn't meet her eyes any longer.

	Her footsteps retreated towards the front door.
PRINCESS:	"It's just—I've been looking at your knives. We'll need something hardier to chop up a boy. A cleaver? I'll go to the town you talked about. Be back just after nightfall if I leave now."
WITCH:	I nodded, not entirely sure what I was agreeing to. "There's some money in the cupboard to your left, the one with…"

The silver hands had raced across the table and were climbing up my torso, digging painfully into my flesh as they crawled. I tried to wrench them away, but my arm muscles were weak from that angle and the fingers sank into my stomach and breasts too deep.

Within two seconds the cold metal was wrapped around my neck, still covered in traces of cookie dough.

The thumbs were pressed tight into my œsophagus. My lips opened in a continuous gasp. I struggled, bashing the hands against the edge of the table, but they held fast. My vision blurred.

The last thing I saw was the girl, her arms prying at my wrists. She called my name like she meant it.

QUEEN:	Their eighth brother had been polishing an antique lamp when he suspected his sister's death. He felt his brothers' sadness as a dull ache at the bottom of his spine, and the rumour spread whip-quick through the perfumed city streets.

Another prince, fully-grown and in search of a wife, heard the story of a princess in a locked glass box and the old man who might own it. But that same old man would disclose nothing of its location or secrets, and the strange-shaped boy beside him whispered that he could take them there if he were not bound to his master.

The older prince slit the old man's throat in one fluid motion. He held out a calloused hand to the shaking boy and said,

PRINCESS: "I am your master now."

WITCH: When I woke, it was surreal.

I was lying on top of the bed, the woollen blanket scratching against my naked back. My arms were wrenched to either side of the mattress. The silver hands were out of sight, and tugging confirmed that they were both tied securely under the bed.

The girl had removed my dress and was straddling my hips, wiping my cuts with a rag soaked in green liquid. The rag stung like being sliced up all over again.

Absinthe, then.

There were perhaps two dozen cuts staggered over my torso. The girl attended to one just next to my nipple and my chest shuddered. She glanced up, registered I was awake and averted her gaze.

PRINCESS: "Apologies. There was..."

WITCH: "You don't have to apologise." My voice came out hoarse and scratchy, followed by a coughing fit.

The girl left to fetch a glass of water. As she went, her thigh brushed over my hip. My mind felt ill and unanchored, like I'd come down with a fever, but I didn't think I had. Thoughts arrived as if through a fog.

Sipping was awkward, with her hand behind my head and the cup at my lips. I took tiny, restricted swallows and trails of water ran down the sides of my mouth. She wiped them aside with her thumb.

"What did you tie them up with?"

PRINCESS: "I found rope in a kitchen cupboard."

WITCH: "It won't hold them much longer. An hour or two, maybe. They'll slice through it. They've hollowed out chunks of my mattress."

Her face fell; her hand holding the cup shook. She turned away to gather her composure.

Three long, fresh scabs ran down her forearm.

Eventually, she said:

PRINCESS: "Well, what else will hold them? Anything here?"

WITCH: "Chains would," I said. "I have none. The mattress might for another hour, longer if they thought that wasn't going to be permanent."

She played with her fingernails while she considered this. Glanced under the bed, then climbed on and reclaimed her position over my hips.

PRINCESS: "I was going to…"

WITCH: She leaned forward, biting her lip, and touched my elbows, making a sawing motion with her fingers.

PRINCESS: "But there's no time."

WITCH: I nodded. The axe. The cleaver. "How did you tie them up at all?"

PRINCESS: "Oh. I wasn't planning to. But once you passed out, they went limp for a while. I don't think they want you dead." *(beat)* "Really dead."

WITCH: When she didn't get a response, the girl picked up the rag and the absinthe again.

PRINCESS: "I know it seems a bit redundant. But may I?"

WITCH: My mouth felt too dry. "Alright."

Her wipes with the rag were gentle and precise. She rested her other hand on my arm, my shoulder, my ribs for balance. Her skin felt twice as soft and warm as my own. Sometimes, she traced my many scars with a fingertip.

Despite myself, my tears started to fall.

She kissed them from the sides of my face, her lips like velvet. She kissed my forehead, my cheeks, my mouth. I felt like I was floating up out of my body, and the stinging faded to background noise. There was no mattress, no rope, no silver hands.

Then her own tears fell onto my collarbone.

PRINCESS: "Is there anything we can do for you?"

WITCH: ...she whispered.

PRINCESS: "Anything at all?"

WITCH: When the words finally came, my voice was cold and composed. Not quite my own.

"We have to cook the boy," I said. *(she lights her candle)*

QUEEN: The prince's men hauled the frosted glass coffin out into the sunlight. The body inside it slipped about—it only occupied about half the space—and for a moment the prince entertained second thoughts. Nonetheless he adjusted his finest coat, turned the key until it clicked in the lock, and raised the lid.

When the prince collapsed inside the coffin, he fit perfectly.

His men locked the coffin with both bodies inside. They were to be buried together, Snow White in a white silk dress and the prince in his suit. A marriage, but not the kind he had been seeking.

WITCH: Inside the oven, the fire blazed. Flames of a million different yellows and oranges licked at the bricks. The boy had been fed and watered. The girl had prepared the lemon-scented cookie dough for baking.

The hands were almost humming in anticipation.

	I willed my pulse to slow and turned to the girl. "It's time."
PRINCESS:	When she woke there was a void in the room. It was a person-shaped void, and the Light Princess believed the king and queen must have lied. She leapt towards it and flesh materialised out of the darkness in her hands.
QUEEN:	The queen bent over her bed, overwhelmed with memories of holding her daughter in that same place for years. She could practically feel Snow White's warm skin against her cheek. The old words slipped unbidden from her lips, and the mirror said:
WITCH:	"You are, my queen."
QUEEN:	...and broke her heart.
WITCH:	She looked me straight in the eyes, so blatantly that I was worried a silver finger would impale me.
PRINCESS:	"Are you sure?"
WITCH:	"Yes. Check that the oven is hot enough, will you?"
	She tugged open the oven door. The girl peered inside, the flames playing over her lovely face.
PRINCESS:	"I don't know how to,"
WITCH:	...she lied.

I blurted out the first curse I could think of. "Let me, then." I shuffled over and took her place, my heart inside my mouth.

I stuck my head clear inside the oven. Further than necessary. So close that the fire sparked in my hair and I could feel my face beginning to burn.

"It's ready," I called.

And she shoved me inside, where the world was white hot.

QUEEN: *(lights her candle)* Eight identical boys whistled as they stepped off their front porch. They were together again, and it was time to settle an old score. The eighth boy had retrieved a pair of crimson shoes from the basement. He knew most of the cottage's contents from his travels, but these shoes seemed especially fitting.

Their mother must be dancing on their sister's grave.

And the queen could dance until she died.

WITCH: My last thoughts were a series of cluttered imaginings: that the girl and her brother ran home, their arms full of candies and treasures and coins.

That they left the remains of the gingerbread house behind them: a smoking pile of powdery ash.

That they arrived, safe, to loving parents.

And that somewhere, the devil appeared to a father who bargained a daughter he forgot could be behind his mill.

It was a small comfort. To know I wasn't the only one.

And the silver hands didn't burn at all.

PRINCESS: *(blows out her candle)* That flesh was cold and strong and pitch, pitch black. In the presence of the void, her heat and her light had retreated to a soft glow, and the Light Princess no longer had to squint to see around her. For the first time, she could just make out the shape of her nose where it sat on her face. She could see her hands for the first time, where they clutched at the void's back. She could see the void's long black hair and short black dress.

WITCH: "You're so warm,"

PRINCESS: ...said the Dark Princess, and even the whites of her eyes were black.

The Light Princess counted to three. / Seven.

QUEEN: The queen could dance / until she died.

WITCH: The silver hands didn't burn at all.

PRINCESS: Twelve.

Neither let go.

Several seconds of silence.

The Witch and The Queen blow out their candles.

END

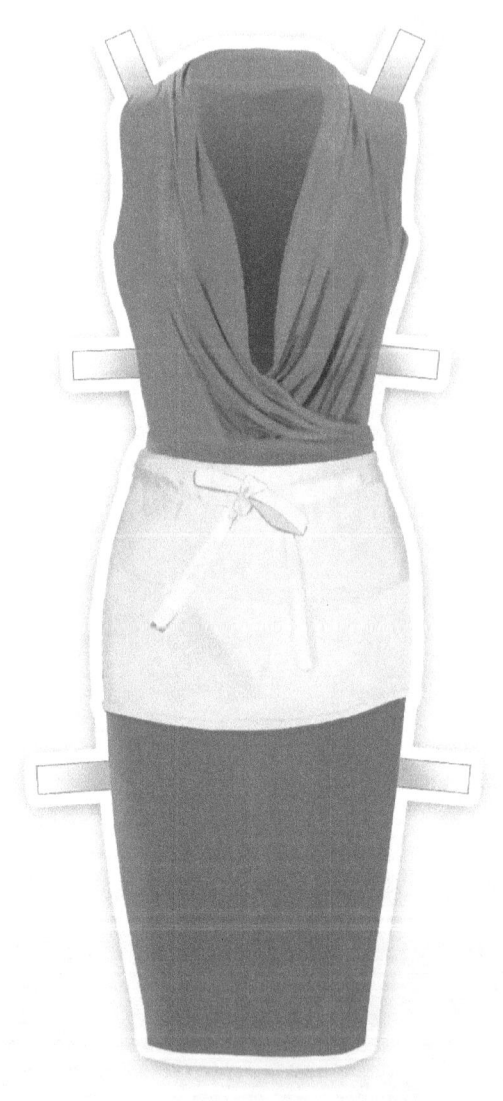

SIR SANTINO AND THE EXCESSIVE CUT-TO

CHARACTERS (in order of appearance):

SANTINO: A childlike king.
NINJAS: Who sneak around and kill cattle.
JOHN WOODHAUS: An executive assistant.
MARY: A cow owner.
ELSEBETH: Fairly low in empathy.
PETER: Kind of a jerk.
VARIOUS VILLAGERS
REX HOLT: A glossy salesperson.
WRITER: The writer of this play.
MRS WOODHAUS: Woodhaus's mother.
CHARLES: Santino's brother.
HELENA: A transition... fairy/god/elf/power-being... thing.
SOPHIA: The ruler of a neighbouring kingdom.

SETTING:

Not our world, but with approximately the same technology as our early twenty-first century.

A NOTE ON FORMATTING & THE CUT-TOS:

Whenever 'cut-to's occur in this play, the original scene is no longer visible and the audience's attention should be completely focused on the new scene. In this way, the 'cut-to's should function as similarly as possible to those in film. Most 'cut-to's are brief interludes—short dalliances from the main narrative—where the return to the original scene is noted using the text 'Back to Scene.' This script was written with the intention that these 'cut-to's would be produced through snap lighting changes across different sections of the stage, but viable deviations from this are welcome.

Lyrics/singing are indicated by dialogue lines in all-capitals.

ACT ONE

- **SCENE ONE**

Darkness. SANTINO clears his throat.

SANTINO: May I have some light, please?

There is light. SANTINO (30s) sports a long white beard.

SANTINO: Thank you. Can you see me?

He moves to the left.

SANTINO: Can you see me now?

He moves farther away.

SANTINO: What about now?

CUT TO

Ninjas. Doing ninja things.

NINJAS: Ninja. Ninja, ninja, ninja.

BACK TO SCENE

SANTINO: What about now?

WOODHAUS: *(offstage)* Yes, sir.

CUT TO

The ninjas.

NINJAS: Ninjas, ninjas, ninjas.

BACK TO SCENE

WOODHAUS enters. Mid-20s. Straight-laced.

WOODHAUS: I do wish you wouldn't cut-to while we're broadcasting, sire.

CUT TO

A small group of villagers including MARY, ELSEBETH and PETER.

MARY: Has anyone seen Milky? Milky?! Oh, I simply must find my cow before the festival!

ELSEBETH: I saw Milky by the stream, Mary.

PETER: I saw Milky under that patch of brambles, Mary.

ELSEBETH: Ha-ha, word.

BACK TO SCENE

WOODHAUS: The villagers find it very distracting when you do that.

SANTINO: And I find it very boring when I don't.

CUT TO

Ninjas appearing next to the villagers.

NINJAS: Ninjas stole Milky!

ELSEBETH: Ha-ha, word!

BACK TO SCENE

WOODHAUS: Well, now you're just being annoying.

SANTINO: I am not. Everyone loves my cut-tos. Cut to me being the most popular king in the galactic empire.

WOODHAUS: Actually, recent polls have found entertainment value in your cut-tos has dropped 70 per cent. Privacy invasion has risen 95 per cent and general disgruntlement has risen 112 per cent.

SANTINO: 112 per cent is not a number.

WOODHAUS: It *is* a legitimate number when—

CUT TO

Glossy salesperson REX.

REX: Is your executive assistant becoming excessively irritating? Purchase our new super product amazement, Assistant in a Box. Download all your assistant's memories into this robot without the annoying personality.

BACK TO SCENE

WOODHAUS: Thank you, sire.

SANTINO makes a disgruntled noise.

WOODHAUS: Look, we all know you're only doing this because of—

SANTINO: Don't!

WOODHAUS: Because of—

SANTINO: Don't!

Silence.

WOODHAUS: Sympathy extends to you, sire, but honestly, your cut-tos are becoming excessive.

Silence.

SANTINO: Okay, so I'll admit that my cut-tos may have gotten a little more frequent after Sophia.

CUT TO

SANTINO on his knees.

SANTINO: SO-PHI-A!

CUT TO

WOODHAUS interrupts the WRITER, who is sitting with their back to the audience.

WOODHAUS: You can't call her—

WRITER: Why not?

WOODHAUS: Well, Sophia is—

WRITER: A name that I hate.

WOODHAUS: But—

WRITER: The powers that be say her name is Sophia!

WOODHAUS: Oh, ok— *(the last half of the word okay is cut off)*

BACK TO SCENE

SANTINO: So I just need to do something fresh with my cut-tos.

Silence.

CUT TO

WOODHAUS and the WRITER.

WOODHAUS: You don't think this is too much of an in-joke?

WRITER: No. *This* is an in-joke.

CUT TO

MARY: Pig!

PETER: Bleach!

SANTINO runs to them, laughing hysterically.

BACK TO SCENE

SANTINO: Oh, my. Hilarious.

CUT TO

WOODHAUS: Ways to travel to the centre of the earth. First, purchase a large drill made of dynamite. Then—

BACK TO SCENE

SANTINO: I know how to make my cut-tos exciting again!

CUT TO

MARY: Pig!

CUT TO

PETER: Bleach!

CUT TO

WOODHAUS: Drill...

CUT TO

ELSEBETH: Milky...

CUT TO

NINJAS: NINJAS!

BACK TO SCENE

Silence.

SANTINO: Wasn't that exciting?!

WOODHAUS: Not really, no.

SANTINO: But I did a whole bunch of them together.

WOODHAUS: I saw what you did there. It doesn't actually make them any better.

SANTINO: It doesn't actually make *you* any better.

WOODHAUS: What?

SANTINO: It doesn't actually make *ya mum* any better.

WOODHAUS: *(genuine)* I know.

Silence.

CUT TO

SANTINO bashing a cushion against the floor.

CUT TO

SANTINO meeting MRS WOODHAUS (MRS W).

SANTINO: Hello, Mrs Woodhaus.

MRS W: Hello, Santino.

SANTINO: How are you today?

MRS W: I'm quite well. How's your beard?

SANTINO: I think it's well. How's your beard?

Silence. She doesn't have one.

BACK TO SCENE

SANTINO: What sort of a name is 'Woodhaus,' anyway?

WOODHAUS: Sire?

SANTINO: I'm going to call you… John.

WOODHAUS: That is my name, sire.

SANTINO: I thought your name was Woodhaus.

WOODHAUS: My name is John Woodhaus.

SANTINO: Oh.

Significant pause. SANTINO starts shuffling playing cards.

WOODHAUS: Sire?

SANTINO: What?

WOODHAUS: You didn't cut-to.

SANTINO: Huh?

WOODHAUS: That means you're getting better!

SANTINO: Yeah?

WOODHAUS: Oh, sire, I'm so sorry, your cut-to-ing was just becoming so prolific and I've done something terrible!

CUT TO

MARY chasing after NINJAS.

MARY: You'd better give Milky back, you bastards! Bring Milky to me!

BACK TO SCENE

SANTINO: Tell me, very carefully, what it is that you have done.

WOODHAUS: I... invited... your brother Charles?

Silence.

Darkness.

CUT TO

SANTINO screaming in horror:

SANTINO: CHAR-LIE!

                          BACK TO SCENE

SANTINO hands WOODHAUS a guitar.

SANTINO: Apologise to me. Apologise. Sing it. And you'd better not lie like last time. Song is supposed to be the most honest aural medium!

WOODHAUS begins to play.

WOODHAUS: I'M SORRY, SANTINO
            I NEVER MEANT TO HURT YOU
            THE VILLAGERS WERE JUST GETTING
            SO SICK OF ALL YOUR CUT-TOS
            NOW CHARLIE'S COMING 'ROUND
            AND YOU KNOW I WON'T DESERT YOU
            I'M SO SORRY, SANTINO
            I LOVE YOU

                              CUT TO

SANTINO: CHAR-LIE!

                          BACK TO SCENE

SANTINO: Maybe I shouldn't do cut-tos any more.

                              CUT TO

VILLAGERS celebrating madly.

VILLAGERS: Yay!

ELSEBETH notices they are in a cut-to.

ELSEBETH: Oh, crap.

                          BACK TO SCENE

WOODHAUS: Maybe you shouldn't.

SANTINO: Maybe I shouldn't.

                              CUT TO

VILLAGERS celebrating madly.

VILLAGERS: Yay!

ELSEBETH notices they are in a cut-to.

ELSEBETH: Oh, crap.

BACK TO SCENE

WOODHAUS: Maybe you shouldn't.

SANTINO: Maybe I shouldn't—Charlie!

CHARLES enters.

CHARLES: Hello, little brother.

SANTINO: Hello, Charlie.

CHARLES: How're your transitions?

SANTINO: Efficient. Yours?

CHARLES: Thought-provoking.

FADE TO

SANTINO and CHARLES as small children.

SANTINO: Give me my teddy.

CHARLES: No.

SANTINO: Give me my teddy.

CHARLES: No.

SANTINO: GIVE ME MY TEDDY!

CHARLES: NO!

BACK TO SCENE

SANTINO makes a disgruntled noise.

SANTINO: I wish you wouldn't do that.

CHARLES: Do what?

> FADE TO

CHARLES with MARY and ELSEBETH.

MARY: Marry me, Charles!

ELSEBETH: Sleep with me, Charles!

MARY: Have my grandmother's ashes, Charles!

> BACK TO SCENE

SANTINO: Okay, so I *know* that was a fantasy and not a memory or a dream.

CHARLES: How do you know?

SANTINO: 'Cos of the lighting and the fuzziness.

CHARLES: All three of those options have the lighting and the fuzziness.

> CUT TO

SANTINO brandishes a wooden spoon at PETER.

SANTINO: You think this is your spoon? This is my goddamn spoon. Goddamit!

> BACK TO SCENE

SANTINO makes a disgruntled noise.

CHARLES: Look, I know ever since Sophia you've been kind of down…

> CUT TO

SANTINO: SO-PHI-A!

BACK TO SCENE

CHARLES: But man, you weren't even with the girl. And she stole your bike.

SANTINO: She did not.

CHARLES: Yeah, she did.

SANTINO: She did not.

CHARLES: See, this is why I could never talk to you properly.

SANTINO: This is why I could never talk to *ya mum* properly.

CHARLES: Dude, my mum is your mum.

Silence.

SANTINO makes a disgruntled noise.

FADE TO

10-year-old SANTINO sits with MARY.

MARY: Santi, you're gonna be the best king ever.

SANTINO: Yeah.

FADE TO

10-year-old SANTINO sits with ELSEBETH.

ELSEBETH: Santi, you're gonna be the best king ever.

SANTINO: Yeah.

FADE TO

10-year-old SANTINO sits with REX.

REX: Santi, you're gonna be the best king ever!

SANTINO: Yeah!

BACK TO SCENE

SANTINO: Okay, okay, I can't take it any more!

SANTINO flings his crown off and exits the stage.

CHARLES picks up the crown, puts it on.

CHARLES: Well, that was convenient.

CUT TO

WOODHAUS in his boxers.

WOODHAUS: What the?

BACK TO SCENE

SANTINO laughs loudly from offstage.

END OF ACT ONE

ACT TWO

- **SCENE TWO**

A forest clearing. WOODHAUS and SANTINO sit around a fire.

WOODHAUS: Don't you like your beans?

SANTINO: No.

WOODHAUS: Look, I told you I was sorry. You don't have to sulk.

SANTINO pokes WOODHAUS with a stick.

SANTINO: I'm not sulking.

CUT TO

SANTINO poking WOODHAUS with a stick in a marginally different position.

BACK TO SCENE

SANTINO: It's boring here. Who knew things outside the castle were so boring?! I know what we need! Women!

CUT TO

A line of dancing WOMEN. At the front is HELENA.

They dance a brief, dramatic finale.

BACK TO SCENE

SANTINO: That. Was. Awesome.

WOODHAUS: It was okay, I guess.

SANTINO: Woodhaus. I know what I have to do.

WOODHAUS: To do? You've fled your throne—the kingdom—all you should be concerned with is staying alive!

SANTINO: I have to travel to England and find that woman.

WOODHAUS: What?

SANTINO: I will find her and woo her and we will have millions of babies.

CUT TO

SANTINO and HELENA locked in a dramatic embrace. HELENA looks a bit shell-shocked.

SANTINO: Darling, where is child number 1,553?

HELENA: Why... I don't know.

SANTINO: Why, let us go to bed and make a million more!

BACK TO SCENE

SANTINO: Wouldn't that be smashing?

WOODHAUS: You use the word 'smashing' now?

SANTINO: I'm trying to be English.

WOODHAUS: You're trying to be *insane*.

SANTINO: Your *mum* is trying to be insane.

WOODHAUS: Sire.

SANTINO: Yes?

CUT TO

MRS W: Would you like some more tea, Santino?

SANTINO: Yes, please, Mrs Woodhaus.

MRS W:	Would you like some cookies, Santino?
SANTINO:	Yes, please, Mrs Woodhaus.
MRS W:	Would you like to get out of my house, jump in a ditch, and get ravaged by a bunch of rabid dogs, Santino?

Silence.

BACK TO SCENE

SANTINO:	I'm going to England!
WOODHAUS:	You don't even know if this woman exists! You just made her up out of the air! How do you know she's in England?!
SANTINO:	Because I know.
WOODHAUS:	No, you don't!

CUT TO

WOODHAUS with his trousers down.

BACK TO SCENE

SANTINO:	Because I know.

Silence.

WOODHAUS:	When do we leave?

▪ SCENE THREE

A dance club. SANTINO spots HELENA.

SANTINO:	My love! Now that we have found each other there is no need to ever breathe another breath out of unison!
HELENA:	Oh. Right. You're the guy.

SANTINO: That's right! I'm *the* guy!

HELENA: I mean you're the guy from the cut-tos.

SANTINO: Yes!

HELENA: You're to come with me.

CUT TO

SANTINO, elated, high-fiving PETER and REX.

SANTINO: Ha-ha. Come.

BACK TO SCENE

HELENA drags SANTINO across the stage to her home.

CUT TO

SANTINO and HELENA in a dramatic embrace.

SANTINO: And we shall go back to our bed and have millions of babies!

He tries to kiss her. She slaps him.

BACK TO SCENE

SANTINO has really been slapped.

SANTINO: You slapped me! How did you do that?

HELENA: With my hands.

SANTINO: But you did it in the cut-to.

HELENA: Yes.

SANTINO: No one's ever been able to do that before! *(beat)* You truly must be my soulmate!

CUT TO

SANTINO and HELENA in a dramatic embrace.

SANTINO: Millions of babies!

He tries to kiss her. She slaps him.

BACK TO SCENE

SANTINO: Ow! Goddamit, that hurts!

HELENA: Then don't do it!

SANTINO: If you weren't put on this green earth to have millions of babies with me, then why are you here?

CUT TO

NINJAS sneaking around the stage.

NINJAS: Ninjas, ninjas, ninjas.

BACK TO SCENE

HELENA: I'm here for that.

CUT TO

MARY tied up.

MARY: Come back here, ninjas! Bring back Milky!

BACK TO SCENE

SANTINO: For what?

HELENA: For that.

CUT TO

NINJAS: Ninjas.

BACK TO SCENE

HELENA: That.

CUT TO

MARY: Milky!

BACK TO SCENE

HELENA: That.

CUT TO

NINJAS: Ninjas!

BACK TO SCENE

HELENA: That.

CUT TO

NINJAS: NINJAS!

CUT TO

HELENA slaps SANTINO.

HELENA: That!

BACK TO SCENE

SANTINO: Ow!

Silence.

SANTINO: I really need to pee. Is that cool?

HELENA sighs dramatically.

HELENA: Oh, okay.

SANTINO exits. HELENA amuses herself by whistling and making a card tower.

Eventually SANTINO returns.

SANTINO: You want to know what happened to me the other day?

> CUT TO

PETER apprehends SANTINO on the street.

PETER: I screwed a penguin.

SANTINO: Awesome?

PETER: Yeah. How many people can claim to screw a penguin! And now I'm banned from the national park!

> BACK TO SCENE

HELENA: You get distracted extremely easily. From now on, you only get five cut-tos a day.

SANTINO gasps.

> CUT TO

SANTINO in prison.

> CUT TO

HELENA in a witch's hat.

> CUT TO

SANTINO dead on the floor.

> CUT TO

HELENA poking SANTINO with a poker.

> CUT TO

SANTINO on his knees.

SANTINO: No-o-o-o-o!

> BACK TO SCENE

HELENA: Congratulations. You just used up your five cut-tos for the day.

SANTINO: I am not bound by your rules, heinous witch fiend! I will show you the true power of my cut-tos!

Silence. Nothing.

SANTINO: The power of my cut-tos!

Silence. SANTINO tries very hard to cut-to and ends up looking nauseous and constipated.

SANTINO: I can't cut-to!

HELENA: That's what I told you.

SANTINO: But why?!

HELENA: Because. I'm a transition... fairy/god/elf/power-being.... thing.

SANTINO: You're a transition... thing.

HELENA: Yes. We never really worked out the appropriate title.

SANTINO: Oh.

HELENA: And you, Santino, are in danger of tearing the universe apart with all your reckless transitions.

SANTINO: But they're so entertaining! I mean, did you see the ninjas? "Ninjas, ninjas, ninjas."

HELENA: Yes. *(pause)* Eat your beans.

SANTINO makes a disgruntled noise.

END OF ACT TWO

ACT THREE

- **SCENE FOUR**

SANTINO sits next to WOODHAUS.

SANTINO: So I figure I have two options: I cause her permanent brain damage, or I kill her.

WOODHAUS just looks at him.

SANTINO: Perhaps I could leave that up to chance. Just hit her really hard in the head with a mallet and see what happens.

WOODHAUS blows bubbles through a straw.

SANTINO: That'd teach her for threatening my masculinity.

Silence.

WOODHAUS: Sire, have you ever thought that this could actually be to your advantage? I mean, everyone used to love your cut-tos. Before they started to get excessive, after—

SANTINO clamps his hand over WOODHAUS's mouth.

SANTINO: Don't say it!

SANTINO removes his hand.

WOODHAUS: After—

SANTINO replaces his hand.

SANTINO: Don't!

SANTINO removes his hand.

WOODHAUS: You mean I'm not *ever* allowed to say 'Sophia?'

CUT TO

SANTINO on his knees.

SANTINO: SO-PHI-A!

BACK TO SCENE

WOODHAUS: Seriously? Every time—

SANTINO: If you say her name again, I will pull your intestines out by your neck and tie them in a bow around your feet.

WOODHAUS makes a disgruntled noise.

WOODHAUS: All I mean is, where do you want to be in two years? Do you have any long term plans? What do you want to do with your life?

SANTINO: Hmmm....

CUT TO

SANTINO, centre stage with a microphone.

SANTINO: Whattup Seattle?!

Roaring applause.

SANTINO: Are we having fun tonight?!

Roaring applause.

SANTINO: Now, I'm gonna do something a little different tonight—I'm gonna tell you the story of my life—through song, jelly and puppets. Yeah!

Roaring applause. SANTINO takes off his shirt and throws it into the audience. Underneath he is wearing an identical shirt.

Random voices offstage shout "take it off", "we love you, Santino" etc.

BACK TO SCENE

SANTINO: Yeah, you know I am.

Silence.

WOODHAUS: Sire, please try to understand. Rock star is not a viable profession for an ex-king with the emotional maturity of a six-year-old.

SANTINO: I'd say that would make me a perfect candidate.

WOODHAUS: I just worry about you...

SANTINO: Well, don't worry about me.

WOODHAUS: But I do. I've missed you and your cut-tos over the past couple of days. I didn't think I ever would, but now that they're gone, life's a lot less colourful. I think you need to get them back.

SANTINO and WOODHAUS look at each other.

CUT TO

MARY and ELSBETH run around SANTINO and WOODHAUS, showering them with rose petals.

MARY: Queer!

ELSEBETH: Gay!

MARY: Homoeroticism, yay!

ELSEBETH: Yay!

MARY: Santino-Woodhaus OTP!

ELSEBETH: Slash!

MARY: Sweaty man-love!

ELSEBETH: Yay!

MARY: Yay!

BACK TO SCENE

Silence. SANTINO looks uneasy.

SANTINO: So I'm thinking I really need to get her back.

WOODHAUS: You never had her in the first place.

SANTINO: Then I should really get her in the first place.

WOODHAUS: Even if she stole your bike.

SANTINO: Sophia did not steal my bike!

CUT TO

SANTINO with a guitar. He sings:

SANTINO: LISTEN UP NOW
SHE DIDN'T STEAL MY BIKE
I'VE STILL GOT MY BIKE
AND IT'S IN MY GARAGE
SOPHIA'S THE HOTTEST CHICK IN THE LAND
SHE DON'T GOT MY BIKE
'COS IT'S IN MY GARAGE

I'M GONNA WIN HER HEART
NOW'S A VERY GOOD TIME TO START
BUT DON'T YOU GODDAMN SAY SHE STOLE MY BIKE

BACK TO SCENE

SANTINO: You know what this means, Woodhaus? I've used up my five cut-tos for the day. I can see Sophia without going—

WOODHAUS: SO-PHI-A!

SANTINO: Yes. Yes, that is correct.

WOODHAUS: You want to go see her now?

SANTINO: I would, but I promised Helena I'd be home for dinner.

Silence.

WOODHAUS: I wish I had a cut-to right now.

- **SCENE FIVE**

SANTINO sits at HELENA's table. HELENA is doing kitchen chores.

SANTINO: Helena, my love, how has your day been?

HELENA: Acceptable.

SANTINO: And why has it not been the best day ever, showered with daisies and sunshine and puppy dogs?

HELENA: Because you've been in it, Santino.

SANTINO: You know what your problem is? You know what everyone's problem is? You've forgotten how to love. You've forgotten how to express emotion!

CUT TO

SANTINO grabbing WOODHAUS by the shoulders.

SANTINO: Your cat died! Its brains were sprayed all over the road! Doesn't that make you feel anything?! Doesn't that make you want to cry like a little girl?!

No reaction from WOODHAUS.

SANTINO: React in some way, you ultimate monster of stone! Why won't you love? Why won't you *love*?!

BACK TO SCENE

SANTINO: And that is why I have a phobia of clowns in coconut hats.

Silence.

SANTINO: Look, is there any way you'd consider lifting this horrible limitation off my pure, innocent shoulders?

HELENA: Well... It takes 28 days to develop a habit. It's been six days so far. I guess if you can get through the next 22 days without whinging or calling me a heinous witch-fiend, I'll remove the curse.

SANTINO: So you admit it's a curse!

HELENA: You know, you've become a lot more bearable and moderate already.

SANTINO: Yeah, you think so?

HELENA: I really do.

SANTINO looks thrilled for a moment.

Silence.

CUT TO

HELENA pokes SANTINO with a poker.

SANTINO: I'm developing Stockholm syndrome! Heinous witch-fiend!

BACK TO SCENE

SANTINO: What I call you in cut-tos doesn't count.

HELENA: It most certainly does.

SANTINO: What I call you for the rest of the day doesn't count.

HELENA: It most certainly does.

SANTINO: Please! Please have mercy on my soul! Open your heart! Give me another chance!

HELENA: Oh, for goodness sake...

SANTINO: PLEASE!

HELENA: Eat your beans.

- **SCENE SIX**

A montage. Upbeat music plays. Cut-tos between all of the following:

A) SANTINO eats his beans.

B) MARY chases the NINJAS.

C) HELENA does the kitchen chores.

D) SANTINO drinks a beer with WOODHAUS.

E) PETER and ELSEBETH dance.

F) REX adjusts SANTINO's tie.

G) HELENA pours tea for the dancing women.

H) NINJAS brush the lint off SANTINO's suit.

I) SANTINO catches HELENA by surprise and kisses her. She doesn't slap him.

Music stops.

SANTINO: Ow!

HELENA: I didn't do anything.

SANTINO: Oh.

They grin at each other.

REX: Are you ready to get your girl back? All dressed up and raring to go? Going to woo her with your snazzy suit? Journeying to bear your soul? With Rex Holt's Win the

       Girl Course 2.0, you're almost guaranteed to not make a complete fool of yourself.

SANTINO: Well, that's good to know.

SANTINO and HELENA look at each other. An awkward moment.

HELENA: Well, it's day 28. I've taken all the restrictions off you.

SANTINO: Thank you.

HELENA: Good luck.

SANTINO: Thank you.

Silence.

WOODHAUS enters.

WOODHAUS: Santino, this wild boar I've tamed won't wait forever. Come on, before it gets sick of eating the dead cow I found by the side of the road. It had this collar around its neck that was oddly familiar, that said 'Milky...'

MARY: *(Off stage)* No-o-o-o-o!

SANTINO: Well, I'll see you 'round and stuff.

HELENA: Yeah.

SANTINO and WOODHAUS exit. Darkness.

- **SCENE SEVEN**

SANTINO and WOODHAUS have been waiting for some time. SANTINO shuffles a pack of cards.

WOODHAUS: She sure does like to keep you waiting.

SANTINO: Yeah. I guess I kind of deserve it...

WOODHAUS: You didn't really do that much wrong, Santino. I mean, you can be a pain in the arse sometimes...

SOPHIA enters. She is only wearing a towel.

SANTINO spots her.

CUT TO

SANTINO on his knees.

SANTINO: SO-PHI-A!

BACK TO SCENE

SANTINO: Oh, goddammit!

SOPHIA: I was in the shower, Santino. What do you want?

SANTINO: I wanted to ask you ice skating on Saturday.

SOPHIA: Now? Santino, I'm busy trying to run my own country. Did you know that there's a bunch of cow-stealing ninjas running around? I haven't seen you for weeks. Are you still doing those infuriating cut-tos?

SANTINO: Less. A lot less.

SOPHIA: Well, I don't know. Ask me later.

SANTINO: Wait a minute! Don't you think my cut-tos are just the least bit funny?

SOPHIA: Not really.

SANTINO: Because I don't have much more to offer than my humour and love... Unless you'd want me for my ability to produce millions of babies?

CHARLES walks in. Wearing a robe.

CHARLES: Oh, I think she's covered for that.

SANTINO takes an enormous gasp of shock.

FADE TO

SANTINO and CHARLES run at each other with swords and have a mighty battle.

The battle ends with CHARLES holding his sword above SANTINO's throat.

BACK TO SCENE

SANTINO leaps at CHARLES, tackling him to the ground. A brief scuffle. SANTINO steals the crown off CHARLES'S head.

SANTINO: Run, Woodhaus!

They do.

- **SCENE EIGHT**

SANTINO and WOODHAUS walk home casually. SANTINO is happily adjusting the crown on his head.

SANTINO: So I thought, fine. If she doesn't appreciate my humour there are a still lot of people who do.

CUT TO

VILLAGERS celebrating wildly.

VILLAGERS: Yay!

ELSEBETH realises what SANTINO actually said.

ELSEBETH: Wait... What?

BACK TO SCENE

SANTINO: I mean, Helena taught me that I can change. I wasn't the best king ever. But that doesn't mean I'll never be the best king ever.

WOODHAUS:	Good for you, sire.
SANTINO:	How long 'til we get back to the castle?
WOODHAUS:	Only another hour now, sire.
SANTINO:	Yeah. I mean, I'll be a great king. All I need to do is listen.

CUT TO

MARY:	Ninjas stole Milky! Why aren't you helping me?!
ELSBETH:	Wait... What?

BACK TO SCENE

WOODHAUS:	I was impressed with how few cut-tos you initiated with Sophia.
SANTINO:	Yeah. I was, too. I mean, there was a fade-to, but Charlie was responsible for that.
WOODHAUS:	I'm so glad I'm not his assistant.
SANTINO:	I'm so glad ya mum's not his assistant.

Silence.

SANTINO:	Actually, speaking of ya mum, I had a couple of mental cut-tos of her during our talk with Sophia. I just didn't show 'em.
WOODHAUS:	Of my mum?

CUT TO

SOPHIA in front of MRS WOODHAUS.

SOPHIA:	Hello, Mrs Woodhaus.
MRS W:	Hello, Sophia. Aren't you a darling? I just love you to pieces!

They embrace.

SOPHIA: Okay, you let go first.

MRS W: No, you let go first.

SOPHIA: No, you.

MRS W: No, you.

NINJAS run in, breaking them apart.

NINJAS: NINJAS!

BACK TO SCENE

SANTINO: And then I saw this…

CUT TO

HELENA in front of MRS WOODHAUS.

HELENA: Hello, Mrs Woodhaus.

MRS W: Hello, Helena.

HELENA: How are you today?

MRS W: Well, I am within a hundred metres of you, so it's like an army of poisonous lizards are rubbing themselves over my entire body.

HELENA: Why, thank you…

MRS W: It would give me great pleasure to see you strung between two trees, burnt to a crisp and then eaten by a thousand hungry crows.

HELENA slaps her.

HELENA: You had better reduce the number of crows! I'll bake them good in my strawberry pies!

BACK TO SCENE

SANTINO grins.

SANTINO: Yeah...

WOODHAUS: Sophia totally stole your bike.

CUT TO

SOPHIA riding Santino's bike.

SOPHIA: Whee!

BACK TO SCENE

SANTINO: Yeah, she totally did.

Silence.

SANTINO: Hey, weren't we supposed to have some sort of festival tonight?

WOODHAUS reacts more strongly than we've ever seen him react before.

WOODHAUS: Oh my God, the festival!

Oh my God, Milky!

Oh my God, Mary!

Oh my God, ninjas!

WOODHAUS runs off.

SANTINO: *(calling after him)* I'm gonna be late for the festival, okay?

Silence.

SANTINO: I take your silence as approval!

SANTINO runs off in the opposite direction.

- **SCENE NINE**

WOODHAUS finds MARY sitting alone.

WOODHAUS: Mary! Oh, God, I'm so sorry about Milky. I'm so sorry.

MARY: It's okay. These things happen, you know. I mean, one day you're happily milking your best friend, the next it's stolen by ninjas and being eaten by a wild boar.

WOODHAUS: Yeah, about that... Hey, aren't you supposed to have a lamb?

MARY: What?

WOODHAUS: Sorry.

MARY: Nah...

WOODHAUS: I'll get those ninjas, Mary. I will avenge Milky's death. She will not have died in vain.

MARY: I'd rather just try to move on. Is that okay?

WOODHAUS: Oh. Sure.

MARY: Do you want to go have sex?

WOODHAUS: Oh. Sure.

They exit happily.

- **SCENE TEN**

HELENA's kitchen. HELENA is cooking.

SANTINO runs in.

SANTINO: HEL-EN-A!

HELENA: You really don't have to yell, Santino. I can hear you just fine.

SANTINO: Helena! I don't care if we never have millions of babies! We don't even have to have one! I just want to see you every day and have you as my wife!

HELENA: *(reluctantly)* Santino...

SANTINO: PLEASE!

HELENA: Oh, yes, of course I will, you ridiculous man.

They kiss.

Everyone cheers.

- **SCENE ELEVEN**

Darkness.

SANTINO clears his throat.

SANTINO: Can I have some light, please?

There is light.

SANTINO: Thank you. Can you see me?

HELENA: Yes! Keep going.

SANTINO: Thank you.

SANTINO clears his throat.

SANTINO: Citizens of my good and noble home. Our home is good and noble. It survived the pirate invasion, even though we are nowhere near the ocean. It survived the vampire outbreak, because of our noble blood diseases. And mostly recently, it survived a bloody attack from some rogue ninjas.

Silence.

SANTINO: Yeah, I'm not gonna do a cut-to, but a shout out to all my ninjas buddies out there!

MARY: *(offstage)* You bastard!

SANTINO: Errr...

HELENA: Shut up! Keep going!

SANTINO: Yeah. So what I wanted to say was, I'm real psyched to be your king again, and I'm not gonna piss you off as much this time. In fact, I've learnt the error of my ways, and I'm not gonna cut-to any more. Ever.

Silence.

SANTINO: See, I didn't cut-to there.

Yeah. No more cut-tos. Except on extra-special public holidays that I decide on, and on weekends.

Silence. The lights fade.

A scream from off stage.

SANTINO: Welcome to Saturday morning!

Snap to black.

END

SHINING ARMOUR

CHARACTERS (in order of appearance):

KATHRYN: A witch.
VARIOUS SOLDIERS, TRAVELLERS & CITIZENS
GEORGE: A hero.
SERA: Kathryn's daughter.
PENELOPE: A princess.
HENRY: A prince.
RINAYA: George's daughter.
A BARKEEP
A MERCHANT
A PRIEST
FREDERICK: A prince.
FERN: Rinaya's godmother.

SETTING:

Not our world. Not our time.

A NOTE ON FORMATTING:

Lyrics/singing are indicated by dialogue lines in all-capitals.

A forward slash (/) is used to indicate when the next character begins speaking before the first character has finished their line(s). Wherever a forward slash appears inside a character's dialogue, the next character should begin to say their line(s) immediately. This will lead to two characters speaking at the same time for at least a moment; this is wholly intentional and is mandatory for all productions.

SONG LIST:

ACT I

1. "Golden books"
2. "It's gonna be magic"
3. "Better me than anyone else"
4. "Hero in town"
5. "That kind of witch"
6. "Morning"
7. "Kiss the girl"
8. "Damn hard"
9. "The stories"
10. "That kind of witch" (reprise)

ACT II

11. "Everybody dies"
12. "It'll be grand"
13. "Someone I want"
14. "Eighteen"
15. "He's your man"
16. "Free"
17. "Give me the road"
18. "No such thing"
19. "For the love"

ACT ONE

- **SCENE ONE**

Snow falls on the city square.

KATHRYN (28) pushes on a cart laden with magical-looking items. She wears a black patchwork dress and a prosthetic nose.

She clips a black cape into place, finds higher ground and pulls on a witch's hat.

KATHRYN: HEARD OF ME, HEARD OF ME
YOU MAY'VE HEARD OF ME
I'M FROM A PLACE A FEW TOWNS TO THE SOUTH
HEARD OF ME, HEARD OF ME
YOU MAY'VE HEARD OF ME
THEY SAY THAT ANGELS FLY OUT OF MY MOUTH

THEY SAY I CAN HEAL
AND THEY SAY I CAN KILL
I'VE POTIONS AND LOTIONS
AND MOUNTAINS OF SKILL
I MURDERED MY HUSBAND
OR SO THEY BELIEVE
THAT WITCH'S BLOOD RUNS RIGHT INSIDE OF MY SLEEVES

SO TAKE HEED
I WON'T PASS THROUGH AGAIN
ALL OF YOU WOMEN AND ALL OF YOU MEN
THIS BOOK THAT IS GOLDEN AND THICK AND IT SHINES
CONTAINS ALL OF THE TALES THAT YOU'RE DYING TO FIND

FAIRIES AND DRAGONS AND PRINCES WITH SWORDS

KATHRYN: MAGICAL ITEMS AND TREASURE IN HORDES
QUESTING AND RESCUES AND MARRIAGES SWEET
AIN'T IT A SHAME... THAT THE STOCK'S ONLY
THREE

ONE TO THE KING AND THE QUEEN FOR THEIR
SON

She hands the first book to a SOLDIER in front of the castle gates.

KATHRYN: HE'S ONLY JUST TWO AND HIS QUEST'S JUST
BEGUN
ONE TO THE HERO THAT SAVED ME LAST
SUMMER...

She hands the second book to GEORGE (30).

KATHRYN: AND ONE TO MY DAUGHTER WITH LOVE FROM
HER MOTHER

SERA (4) sticks her hand out from inside the cart. Kathryn passes her the final book.

KATHRYN: HEARD OF ME, HEARD OF ME
YOU MAY'VE HEARD OF ME
CART IS STILL LADEN WITH THINGS I CAN SELL
HEARD OF ME, HEARD OF ME
YOU MAY'VE HEARD OF ME
I WON'T BE BACK SO MAKE SURE YOU SPEND WELL

The CITIZENS who have gathered around her thrust forward their money.

- **SCENE TWO**

20 years later.

PENELOPE (17) sits at her piano, reading the Golden Book. She finishes reading, wipes away some tears and begins to play:

PENELOPE: A LONG TIME AGO
IN A REALM FAR AWAY

                LIVED A LAND WITH A KING AND QUEEN
                BUT THINGS WERE NOT SO GREAT UP THERE
                BECAUSE THEY WERE DYING
                BUT EVERYONE, THEY STILL HAD HOPE
                BECAUSE A GIRL LIKE ME
                WOULD COME TO RULE SO VERY SOON
                SHE'S PRINCESS PENELOPE

In her fantasy, a group of citizens rush into the city square to celebrate her.

MEN: I HEARD A RUMOUR
               THE KING AND QUEEN ARE ILL

WOMEN: I HEARD A RUMOUR
               THOUGH THEY ARE ALIVE STILL

CITIZENS: IT WON'T BE LONG
               'TIL OUR PRINCESS COMES ALONG
               SHE'S EVERYTHING WE'VE DREAMED OF
               SHE'S PRETTY, SMART AND WISE
               IT'S GONNA BE, IT'S GONNA BE MAGIC
               WHEN PENELOPE ARRIVES

WOMAN: I'VE ALWAYS KNOWN SHE'D BRING US PEACE
               I'VE ALWAYS KNOWN SHE'D RISE

MAN: BRINGING HAPPINESS TO ALL THE LAND
               UPON THE ROYALS' DEMISE

CITIZENS: IT'S GONNA BE, IT'S GONNA BE MAGIC
               IT'S GONNA BE, IT'S GONNA BE FANTASTIC
               WE'LL BE SO HAPPY FOR YOU
               JUST SO HAPPY FOR YOU
               PENELOPE

Penelope's half-brother HENRY (22) enters. The citizens snap out of Penelope's fantasy and resume their daily business.

HENRY: You're pretty loud.

PENELOPE: My parents are sick. I can be loud.

HENRY: You sounded jaunty.

Silence.

Have you been crying?

PENELOPE: Did that new medicine help at all?

HENRY: No. Nothing helps.

PENELOPE: It helps me, you know, to make my story like one of the fairy tales in the book.

HENRY: I know. That helps me, too.

Silence.

HENRY: What are you going to do once you're queen?

PENELOPE: I haven't really thought about it.

HENRY: *(displeased)* What?

PENELOPE: I mean, I was always going to discuss it with...

HENRY: Yes?

PENELOPE: My husband. But I'm 18 in a month and he still hasn't found me. None of the princesses in that book get married past the age of 18. I'm so near my expiration date.

HENRY: Hey. Our parents are enough to worry about. Your prince will find you.

- **SCENE THREE**

Night-time. A few citizens hurry through the streets with candles, whispering to one another.

George wakes his daughter RINAYA (19).

GEORGE:	Rina. Sweetheart.
RINAYA:	Papa?
GEORGE:	I have to go, sweetheart. Emergency.

He dresses in a light suit of armour.

RINAYA:	What emergency?
GEORGE:	They took Penelope.
RINAYA:	Took her? Who took her?
GEORGE:	We don't know, but she's gone. I don't know how long I'll be, alright, so you know the drill. Take care of yourself and the house 'til I'm back.
RINAYA:	*(knows the answer is no)* Can't I come too, Papa?
GEORGE:	Absolutely not. You know the stories. I'm the hero. Girls get into strife in the forest.
RINAYA:	I'm not like those girls.
GEORGE:	I have to go, love. I gotta save the princess.

He leaves. A cluster of candle-carrying citizens have gathered around his front door. Their whispers grow in volume when they spot him...

...only to finish in gasps and cries when he collapses two metres from his house.

George yells out in pain. Rinaya rushes to the window to watch a couple of citizens help him.

GEORGE:	I swear to God, there was not a trench outside my door earlier tonight.
CITIZEN #1:	Can you walk?

George attempts to put weight on his ankle. He cries out. Henry approaches.

CITIZEN #2: But… we don't have any other heroes!

CITIZEN #3: It's always been George!

CITIZEN #4: What about the princess?

CITIZEN #3: What'll happen to her / now?

HENRY: Citizens! There's no need to panic. I've already dispatched a team of elite soldiers to retrieve the princess. No one wants her back more than I do.

CITIZEN #2: Soldiers aren't heroes!

CITIZENS: Yeah!

RINAYA: WHAT'S A GIRL TO DO
WHEN THE KINGDOM'S GONE BALLISTIC?
WHEN THEY WROTE OFF HER FATHER FOR HIS
BAD LUCK DRAW?

WHAT'S A GIRL TO DO
WHEN THE PRINCESS HAS BEEN CAPTURED?
KIDNAPPED BY THE BAD GUYS JUST MOMENTS
BEFORE?

THERE'S NOTHING THEY CAN DO
THEY DON'T KNOW THE TRICKS OF THE TRADE
(realising) NOT AS WELL AS I DO
I BET I'M WELL EQUIPPED TO SAVE HER HIGHNESS
AS I'M ALMOST TRAINED BY THE HERO
BY THE KNIGHT HIMSELF
OR ELSE BETTER ME THAN ANYONE ELSE

She opens the trunk with George's old suit of armour. She puts it on.

RINAYA: WHO ELSE IS GONNA SAVE HER?
BY THE TIME THEY DECIDE IT'LL BE TOO LATE
NAME A SINGLE BLOKE WHO'S BRAVER
MY SMARTS ARE SURE TO COMPENSATE
CAN'T STAND THAT SHE'S IN DANGER
THIS JOURNEY WILL BECOME MY FATE
AND IT'S BETTER ME THAN ANYONE ELSE!

Rinaya slides the sword onto her back and runs off.

- **SCENE FOUR**

Sera's tower. Penelope struggles out of a sack, her nightie slightly bloodstained. She tries the door, which is locked, and then runs to the window.

PENELOPE: Help! Help!

Penelope bends over the windowsill. Sera (24) enters, wearing her mother's witch outfit. Sera places down a bowl and mug with a loud clunk. Penelope rights herself.

PENELOPE: What do you want with me?

SERA: Nothing.

Penelope inches forward, picks up the mug. Throws its contents in Sera's face.

SERA: Not that kind of witch.

Sera adjusts her prosthetic nose and leaves.

- **SCENE FIVE**

Outside an inn, the BARKEEP brings Rinaya a mug of ale. She wears a luminous glass ring on a string around her neck.

BARKEEP: That'll be two silver pieces.

She pays him.

A MERCHANT is sitting next to her.

MERCHANT: You a hero, kid?

RINAYA: I'm 19.

MERCHANT: Don't see too many heroes.

She ignores him.

MERCHANT: So how long you been travelling for?

RINAYA: A day or so.

MERCHANT: A day? (*laughs*) Wow. Bet you've seen a lot of adventure in a *day*.

RINAYA: I have, actually.

MERCHANT: Yeah? You gonna tell me about it?

Silence.

MERCHANT: Tell you what—you sing me a little song about your adventures, like the real heroes do, and I'll buy you that drink.

They shake on it.

Rinaya stands. Frustrated, she climbs onto the table.

RINAYA: BACK AT HOME
IT USED TO BE
TEND THE FIRE
POUR THE TEA
SEW HIS SHIRTS UP
WASH HIS UNDERWEAR

BUT ALL ALONG
THEY GOT IT WRONG
'COS I'M NOT MEANT FOR CLEANING SONGS
MY DESTINY'S MUCH BIGGER THAN BACK THERE

'COS THERE'S A NEW BREED OF HERO IN TOWN
I'M CUTTING MY TEETH BUT I'M STICKING AROUND
AND WHEN YOU HEAR WHAT I'VE DONE YOU'LL BE PROUD
TO TELL THE WORLD
THERE'S A HERO IN TOWN

MERCHANT: SO WHAT DID YOU DO?

RINAYA: I BURNT A BUNCH OF LEECHES

MERCHANT: WHAT DID YOU DO?

RINAYA: I CUT A SNAKE TO PIECES

MERCHANT: WHAT DID YOU DO?

RINAYA: I STABBED A WOLF RIGHT THERE

She points to her heart.

MERCHANT: AND WHAT DID YOU DO?

RINAYA: I SAVED A BOY FROM DROWNING

MERCHANT: WHAT DID YOU DO?

RINAYA: I FOUND A GLOWING RING AND

MERCHANT: WHAT DID YOU DO?

RINAYA: GOT BLOOD ALL THROUGH MY HAIR

A BOY enters, dripping wet.

BOY: Thanks, lady!

Rinaya gives him the thumbs up.

RINAYA: SO WHENEVER YOU NEED HELP
            YOU KNOW I'LL BE THERE

            BACK AT HOME
            IT USED TO BE
            SWEEP THE CINDERS
            CAN'T YOU SEE
            HANGING ALL THESE CLOTHES
            IS CRUSHING ME

> 'COS THERE'S A NEW BREED OF HERO IN TOWN
> I'M CUTTING MY TEETH BUT I'M STICKING AROUND
> SO REMEMBER WHAT I'VE DONE AND BE PROUD
> TO TELL THE WORLD
> THERE'S A HERO IN TOWN!

Everyone claps—many only because they find her amusing. Rinaya bows anyway. The merchant hands her the silver pieces.

Rinaya enters the inn. She is followed closely by two soldiers.

SOLDIER #1: Wait. You're on a very particular road at a very particular time.

Silence.

SOLDIER #2: What are your intentions?

RINAYA: My intentions? I'm going to save the princess. Your princess. Princess Penelope.

The soldiers glance at each other. They lunge at her.

Rinaya ducks and runs up to the second floor. The guards corner her in front of a window.

SOLDIER #1: Now, now, nowhere to go.

SOLDIER #2: The forest isn't safe for girls like you.

Rinaya climbs onto the window ledge.

SOLDIER #2: Don't do anything rash.

They lunge at her again. She jumps out the second floor window.

- **SCENE SIX**

Through a slit in the tower door, Sera watches Penelope sleep.

Sera shuts the slit and pulls out an expensive piece of parchment.

SERA: *(reading)* "To the Witch of the North-North-East...

I can offer you a large sum of money to imprison a girl in your tower—should you have a tower—for as long as it takes for her rescue. She should not be especially easy to rescue, nor terribly difficult. Nor should she be treated especially well, nor terribly harshly. This is for the ultimate good of the kingdom; I don't know whether this means you are more or less likely to accept my offer, but I assure you your fee shall be more than acceptable."

Of course I have a tower.

She goes to her kitchen and rolls gingerbread dough.

SERA: I'M AWARE OF HER THIRST LIKE A TRICKLE

She bangs her rolling pin—thwack, thwack, thwack, thwack.

SERA: LIKE A BIRD AT MY NECK AND ITS FICKLE
PECK, PECK, PECK, PECK
AND I CAN'T REWARD HER APPALLING BEHAVIOR
CAN'T LET HER STARVE
CAN'T BUDGE AN INCH

Thwack, thwack, thwack, thwack.

SERA: BUT I'M NOT THAT KIND OF WITCH

Thwack, thwack, thwack, thwack, thwack, thwack, thwack.

SERA: PEOPLE SEE
WHAT I CAREFULLY CULTIVATE
TOWER, ME
UGLY MAKEUP AND
BROOM AND HERBS
RUNNING THIS BUSINESS IS
QUITE ABSURD

Thwack, thwack, thwack, thwack, thwack.

SERA: AND THERE'S THE BIRD

Thwack, thwack, thwack, thwack, thwack, thwack, thwack. She puts the gingerbread into the oven.

SERA: NEVER KILLED
NEVER TORTURED
RUN THIS ALL ON TRICKS AND GAMES
ILLUSIONS, SLEIGHT OF HAND
WHAT'S ONE MORE FOR THE DAY?

SO JUST THIS ONCE
I'LL MAKE A CONCESSION
BOTH SAVE HER STOMACH
AND TEACH HER A LESSON
SAID I WOULD NEVER
BUT JUST THIS ONCE
FOR IN A PINCH

She stands in front of her bedroom mirror. She removes her fake nose and black dress. Underneath is a brown slip—she looks like any other girl.

SERA: I AM JUST THAT KIND OF WITCH

Sera goes back to the kitchen, fills a giant mug ¾ with tea and ¼ with a potion, and takes the mug and some cooked gingerbread cookies upstairs.

She checks that Penelope is still sleeping, then enters the tower.

Carefully, Sera wakes Penelope. Sera helps her sit up and holds the tea to Penelope's lips.

SERA: Careful. Don't want to throw it up.

Penelope eats the gingerbread cookies.

PENELOPE: Who are you?

SERA: Sera.

PENELOPE: Are you helping to rescue me?

SERA: No.

PENELOPE:	More drink, please. Do you work for her?
SERA:	No. Who are you?
PENELOPE:	You don't know who I am?

Silence.

PENELOPE:	I'm the princess.

Silence.

PENELOPE:	*What* are you?
SERA:	I'm a ghost, of sorts. I was trapped here years ago, and I got sick. But the witch cursed my soul to stay on.
PENELOPE:	You feel real.
SERA:	I can be. For a little while every night.

Silence.

SERA:	Why were you kidnapped?
PENELOPE:	*(shakes her head)* Everyone loves me. My parents are dying. I have to get home. They can't die while I'm here.
SERA:	My parents are dead. Probably. My father was a magician and my mother was a scientist. One day, in the middle of his act, my father disappeared. They blamed my mother. He never came back.
PENELOPE:	Real magic?
SERA:	As real as it gets.
PENELOPE:	I won't be here for long, you know. I'll be rescued soon.
SERA:	Oh? The others weren't. Like me.
PENELOPE:	But... I'm a princess.

Penelope falls into a drugged sleep.

- **SCENE SEVEN**

A PRIEST stands at a podium in front of the palace.

PRIEST: This is a time for remembrance and reflection, but it is also a time to embrace change. Just as their souls fly upwards towards the heavens...

HENRY waits off to the side.

HENRY: RIGHT OVER THERE
THEY'RE LOOKING SO SOLEMN
ALL EMPTY WORDS
AND TALKING OF COFFINS
AND IF THAT'S HOW IT STARTS
I'M NOT SURE THAT I WANT IT
NOT SURE THAT I WANT IT

RIGHT OVER THERE
THEY'RE SAYING IT'S OVER
RIP MUM AND DAD
COULD IT PASS ANY SLOWER?
THIS MORNING, THIS MORNING
THIS HORRIBLE MORNING
PASSES LIKE A SNAIL

I HAD NO IDEA
WHEN I WENT TO BED LAST NIGHT
THAT THIS MORNING, THIS MORNING
WOULD BE SUCH A SIGHT
'COS THIS MORNING, THIS MORNING
EVERYONE'S MOURNING
I'M SUPPOSED TO TAKE FLIGHT

'COS THAT'S HOW IT WORKS WITH REGENCY
WELL, ISN'T THAT RIGHT?

Henry goes to the podium. The priest crowns him.

HENRY: RIGHT OVER HERE
I'M EXPRESSING MY SORROW
I'M GIVING MY THANKS
AND I'LL MENTION TOMORROW
TOMORROW, TOMORROW
IT'S BETTER TOMORROW
ACCORDING TO ME

RIGHT OVER HERE
THERE'S NO OTHER OPTION
SO I'LL HAVE THE COURAGE
THE STRENGTH AND THE GUMPTION
TO RULE AS YOUR LEADER
YOUR LEADER, YOUR LEADER
FROM NOW ON THIS MORNING

Henry bows and leaves the podium.

HENRY: I HAD NO IDEA
WHEN I WENT TO BED LAST NIGHT
THAT THIS MORNING, THIS MORNING
WOULD BE SUCH A SIGHT
'COS THIS MORNING, THIS MORNING
EVERYONE'S MOURNING
I'M SUPPOSED TO TAKE FLIGHT

George hops awkwardly towards Henry. Two soldiers detain George.

GEORGE: Sir Henry!

Henry motions for the soldiers to release George.

GEORGE: You might have heard. Please. My daughter, Rinaya. She's missing. In the forest, I think. I know this is a difficult time for everyone, but please can't you find her?

HENRY: I can't send out a search party for every missing person.

GEORGE: You sent one for—

HENRY: The princess. And if your daughter is in the forest like you say, they may well find her in the meantime.

GEORGE: Come on, Henry. I'm not just anyone.

HENRY: No, you're not.

GEORGE: I'd find her myself if it weren't for my ankle.

HENRY: Your daughter's an adult, isn't she? Perhaps she doesn't want to be found.

GEORGE: You don't understand. She's very... special. She can't be in the forest.

HENRY: Oh no? Why?

George whispers in Henry's ear.

GEORGE: Will you find her?

HENRY: I'll do more than find her.

Henry leaves.

- **SCENE EIGHT**

A thick rope stretches between Sera's tower window and a nearby tree. Halfway up the tree, Rinaya unhooks a handle from the rope. She climbs down and helps Penelope down after her.

Rinaya pulls Penelope through the forest at a breakneck pace.

PENELOPE: Wait!

They exit. Moments pass. Rinaya pulls Penelope back on stage.

PENELOPE: Wait! You're a girl!

Rinaya pulls Penelope behind a tree.

PENELOPE: And you're supposed to be carrying me.

RINAYA: Please keep your voice down. My father was supposed to come for you, but he injured his ankle. We'd be too slow if I carried you. We're probably being followed.

PENELOPE: You're a girl.

RINAYA: But I rescued you, didn't I?

PENELOPE: I kind of wish you hadn't.

Silence.

RINAYA: Let's keep moving.

Rinaya pulls her along at a swift walk.

PENELOPE: You don't understand. You're supposed to be my husband.

Silence.

PENELOPE: This was my last chance!

Silence. Penelope gasps loudly. Rinaya stops. Penelope beams at her.

PENELOPE: OH, I KNOW WHAT THIS IS
YEAH, I'VE HEARD IT ALL BEFORE
YOU'RE THE HIDEOUS, CRAZY, STUPID THING
THAT I MUST LEARN TO LOVE
AND THEN I KISS YOU
YOU TURN INTO A PRINCE
AND WE GET MARRIED IN A PALACE WITH A STEED

Rinaya stares at her. She reaches for Penelope's hand, but Penelope darts away.

        OH, I KNOW WHAT THIS IS
        YEAH, I'VE SEEN IT ALL BEFORE
        WELL, USUALLY YOU'RE A MONSTER OR A FROG
        OR JUST PLAIN UGLY
        AND A GIRL IS QUITE SUBVERSIVE, BUT—
        WHY ARE YOU LOOKING AT ME LIKE THAT?

>
> MAYBE IF I KISS THE GIRL
> HE'LL TURN INTO WHAT HE SHOULD BE
> MAYBE IF I KISS THE GIRL
> THIS TALE WILL END MORE HAPPILY
> YEAH, I KNOW IT'S NOT QUITE RIGHT
> BUT IF I WANT MY WEDDING NIGHT
> THEN I KNOW WHAT I MUST DO
> MAYBE IF I KISS THE GIRL
> ALL MY DREAMS WILL FINALLY COME TRUE

Penelope grabs Rinaya and kisses her. Rinaya jerks away.

RINAYA: Are you mad?

PENELOPE: Maybe I have to do it again.

RINAYA: I'm not... I'm not cursed.

PENELOPE: OH, I KNOW WHAT THIS IS
YEAH, IT'S VERY CLEAR TO SEE
THAT YOU'RE TOO SHORT, YOUR VOICE IS HIGH
AND YOU HAVE BREASTS
Maybe we could lop them off?
SO WE CAN'T MARRY IN A PALACE WITH A STEED

OH, I KNOW WHAT THIS IS
YEAH, IT'S VERY CLEAR TO ME
THAT ONE MORE KISS SHOULD BREAK THE SPELL
AND FIX YOU UP
AND THIS IS UNEXPECTED
BUT WHY ARE YOU LOOKING AT ME LIKE THAT?

MAYBE IF I KISS THE GIRL
HE'LL TURN INTO WHAT HE SHOULD BE
MAYBE IF I KISS THE GIRL
THIS TALE WILL END MORE HAPPILY
YEAH, I KNOW IT'S NOT QUITE RIGHT
BUT IF I WANT MY WEDDING NIGHT
THEN I KNOW WHAT I MUST DO
MAYBE IF I KISS THE GIRL
ALL MY DREAMS WILL FINALLY COME TRUE

Penelope takes Rinaya in her arms.

PENELOPE: Please let me try again.

RINAYA: Nothing will happen.

PENELOPE: So nothing happens. Let me try?

Penelope kisses her for several seconds. Eventually, Rinaya steps away.

PENELOPE: I think that was long enough. Maybe we have to do it after dark, or at dawn, or... maybe I don't love you enough. I suppose I can work on that.

RINAYA: Maybe we should concentrate on getting somewhere safe.

Rinaya pulls Penelope along again.

PENELOPE: That armour does come off, doesn't it?

RINAYA: Of course, why?

PENELOPE: Maybe I'm kissing you in the wrong place.

A dart hits Penelope in the neck and she collapses.

Rinaya whirls around, drawing her sword.

- **SCENE NINE**

In her witch's outfit, Sera paints some apples with a glassy, sugary liquid.

SERA:
EVERY MORNING
THE CLOCK STRIKES FOUR
AND I SNEAK TO THE TOWER
AND PEER THROUGH THE DOOR
I'VE WIPED OFF MY MAKEUP
AND BARELY LOOK LIKE ME

I STARE THROUGH YOUR WINDOW
AND I'M JUST A GIRL
I BRING SOME SUPPLIES

AND I ENTER YOUR WORLD
WE WHISPER AND LAUGH
TRY NOT TO WAKE—ME

'COS THIS IS SO PERFECT
NO LONGER ALONE
AND I WISH I COULD OPEN
THAT LOCK AND MY HOME

BUT THEN THERE'S REPUTATION
AND IT'S WORTH THE AGGRAVATION
AND THEN THERE'S UNEMPLOYMENT
AND YOU KNOW I DON'T ENJOY IT

Penelope leans out the tower window.

SERA: IT'S DAMN HARD TO MAKE A LIVING

PENELOPE: AHHH, AHHH

SERA: WHEN YOU'RE PAID TO BE A BITCH

PENELOPE: AHHH, AHHH

SERA: NOW I'M STUCK IN THIS PROFESSION

PENELOPE: AHHH, AHHH

SERA: IT'S MY JOB TO BE A WITCH

PENELOPE: AHHH, AHHH

SERA: AND I LOOK AT THE WORLD
AND I HATE WHAT THEY SEE
AND THE MONEY ROLLS IN
BUT I WANT TO BE ME
BUT WHAT ELSE CAN I DO?

IT'S DAMN HARD TO MAKE A LIVING
I'LL CHANGE AT FOUR AM FOR YOU

EVERY MORNING THE CLOCK STRIKES SIX
AND I SNEAK BACK INSIDE
TRANSFORM INTO THE WITCH

I PUT ON MY MAKEUP
AND WONDER IF THAT'S ME

I REMEMBER HER SKIN THAT
I'M SO SCARED TO TOUCH
AND I'M HAUNTED BY EYES
WHO'D DESPISE ME SO MUCH
IF SHE LEARNT THE TRUTH
ABOUT WITCHES, SERA, ME

'COS THIS IS TOO PERFECT
NO LONGER ALONE
AND I WISH I COULD OPEN
THAT LOCK AND MY HOME

BUT THEN THERE'S REPUTATION
AND IT'S WORTH THE AGGRAVATION
AND THEN THERE'S UNEMPLOYMENT
AND YOU KNOW I DON'T ENJOY IT

IT'S DAMN HARD TO MAKE A LIVING

PENELOPE: AHHH, AHHH

SERA: WHEN YOU'RE PAID TO BE A BITCH

PENELOPE: AHHH, AHHH

SERA: NOW I'M STUCK IN THIS PROFESSION

PENELOPE: AHHH, AHHH

SERA: IT'S MY JOB TO BE A WITCH

PENELOPE: AHHH, AHHH

SERA: AND I LOOK AT THE WORLD
AND I HATE WHAT THEY SEE
AND THE MONEY ROLLS IN
BUT I WANT TO BE ME
BUT WHAT ELSE CAN I DO?

IT'S DAMN HARD TO MAKE A LIVING
I'LL CHANGE AT FOUR AM FOR YOU

Sera finishes the bowl of apples.

- **SCENE TEN**

George's house. Rinaya wakes in her bed, thoroughly beaten and bruised. George sits nearby. He coughs, waking her.

RINAYA: Papa?

GEORGE: Rina? Oh, Rina. What have you done to yourself? I've been worried. You've been unconscious for almost a day.

RINAYA: A day? I'm at home?

GEORGE: Yes, honey.

RINAYA: But... I was a week's walk away.

GEORGE: Some soldiers found you at an inn last night. You fell out a window. Do you remember?

RINAYA: Sort of.

GEORGE: I warned you about this, sweetheart. The forest is no place for girls, especially girls like you. It will take some time for you to heal, but I want to you promise me you will never leave the city again.

RINAYA: I... I'm really confused, Papa. I thought I was doing so well.

George helps her sit up. She winces. He coughs.

GEORGE: You hurt?

RINAYA: Everything hurts.

Silence.

RINAYA: How are you, Papa?

GEORGE: Aside from being left alone with a busted ankle, I'm doing fine.

LISTEN MY BABY
LISTEN MY LOVE
I CAN'T HAVE YOU STRAYING OFF INTO THE SHRUB
WHERE YOU'LL BRUISE AND YOU'LL BREAK
AND YOU'LL BLEED ON THE BUGS
AND MY HEART BREAKS

LISTEN MY DARLING
LISTEN MY GIRL
REMEMBER THE STORIES
REMEMBER THE WORDS
THAT SAY "LONG, LONG AGO"
AND "ONCE IN A LOST TIME"
THEY'RE STILL CURRENT TODAY
AND I'LL REFRESH YOUR MIND

THAT THE GIRLS IN THE STORIES
THEY SUFFER AND CRY
WHEN THEY'RE INSIDE THE FOREST
THEY'RE OUT OF THEIR MINDS
'COS THEY'RE CURSED OR THEY'RE TRAPPED
OR THEY'RE EATEN AND DIE
AND THEY'RE NEVER THE HEROES
NOT ONE SINGLE TIME

AND THE GIRLS IN THE STORIES
THEY PINE AND THEY WAIT
AND THERE'S NO WAY MY DAUGHTER
ENDS UP IN THAT STATE
SO YOU'LL PROMISE ME, PROMISE ME
THAT'S NOT YOUR FATE
AND YOU'LL STAY HERE

JUST STAY HERE

STAY WITH ME, DAUGHTER
STAY WITH ME, BELLE
STAY IN THE CITY THAT YOU KNOW SO WELL

                    WHERE YOU'RE SAFE AND YOU'RE SOUND
                    AND YOU'RE FREE FROM THE HELL THAT'S
                    OUTSIDE HERE

                    PROMISE ME, PROMISE ME, PROMISE ME,
                    PROMISE ME
                    PROMISE ME, PROMISE ME, PROMISE ME,
                    PROMISE ME
                    PROMISE ME, PROMISE ME, PROMISE ME,
                    PROMISE ME
                    PROMISE ME, PROMISE ME, PROMISE—

RINAYA: I promise, Papa.

GEORGE: ME

- **SCENE ELEVEN**

At sunrise, FREDERICK (20s) climbs through Sera's tower window with a thump. This alerts Sera, who cleans Penelope's chamber pot just outside the door. Sera watches him through the door's slit.

Frederick kisses Penelope, who does not wake. He starts to remove her nightie, when...

...Sera rushes in and whacks him in the head with the chamber pot. He collapses, bleeding. Sera feels his pulse. Her hands shake.

SERA: NEVER KILLED
                    NEVER TORTURED
                    RUN THIS ALL ON TRICKS AND GAMES
                    ILLUSIONS, SLEIGHT OF HAND
                    WHAT'S ONE MORE FOR THE DAY?

She drags Frederick's body downstairs. On the way down, she notices two soldiers standing outside.

SERA: SO JUST THIS ONCE
                    I'LL MAKE A CONFESSION
                    I'LL TAKE HIS HEART
                    I TAUGHT HIM A LESSON

SAID I WOULD NEVER
BUT JUST THIS ONCE
FOR IN A PINCH

She plunges a knife into his chest and cuts out his heart.

SERA: I AM JUST THAT KIND OF WITCH

END OF ACT ONE

ACT TWO

- **SCENE TWELVE**

Sera watches Frederick's body burn in her oven. She holds his heart wrapped in cloth.

SERA: FIRE, FIRE
          BURNING BRIGHTER
          GROW WITH FLAMES OF RED AND BLUE

She runs into her bedroom.

          MIRROR, MIRROR
          SHOW ME A PICTURE
          OF SOMEONE WHO KNOWS WHAT TO DO

She places the heart, her witch's hat, two urns and a second cloth into a basket.

          COLLECT HIS HEART
          AND COLLECT THE HAT
          COLLECT THE CLOTH
          AND THE JARS OF ASH
          GOODBYE TO ALL I WAS BEFORE
          I SMASHED THE HINGES OFF THAT DOOR

She takes the basket back upstairs.

          CARRY ME UP AND
          CARRY ME QUICK
          WHEN ALL YOUR BRIDGES BURN LIKE WICKS
          THERE'S ONE LAST THING
          THAT ALWAYS FLIES
          THAT EVERYBODY
          EVERYBODY DIES

She dumps the ash from the urns in a pile on the tower floor.

> MOTHER, MOTHER
> FIX MY BLUNDER
> KILL ME SWIFT AND KILL ME SAFE
>
> SISTER, SISTER
> LET'S CONVINCE HER
> SO YOUR DEATHS WERE NOT A WASTE

She drops the witch's hat on top of the ash pile, then wakes Penelope.

PENELOPE: Sera? But it's daylight.

SERA: I know. The witch is dead. The spell is broken.

PENELOPE: What?

SERA: Listen to me very carefully. During the night, a prince came and killed the witch with a potion. But he slipped on the potion and cracked his head open. Before he died, he told me that someone from your palace put you in here. You can't go home. The only way you'll be free is if we fake your death. So we're going to use the prince's heart and say it's yours—that you're dead—understand?

PENELOPE: Not really.

SERA: Okay, give me your nightie. Give me your nightie or you will die.

Penelope takes it off. Sera wraps Frederick's heart in the nightie and hands Penelope the clean cloth.

SERA: Clean up the blood.

Penelope does. Sera runs downstairs with the heart. They sing their next parts simultaneously:

PENELOPE:
> CLEAN UP THE BLOOD
> AND CLEAN UP MY LIFE
> I WAS TO BE A
> QUEEN AND WIFE
> GOODBYE TO ALL I
> WAS BEFORE

SERA:
    WHEN EVERYBODY
    EVERYBODY DIES

SERA: CARRY ME DOWN AND
    CARRY ME QUICK
    WHEN ALL YOUR BRIDGES
    BURN LIKE WICKS
    THERE'S ONE LAST THING
    THAT ALWAYS FLIES
    THAT EVERYBODY
    EVERYBODY DIES

At her front door, Sera passes the soldiers the heart.

- **SCENE THIRTEEN**

Rinaya sneaks out of bed, past a sleeping George, and pulls on her clothes and shoes. She looks slightly bruised but healing nicely.

Simultaneously, Henry examines Frederick's heart.

HENRY: WELL, THIS IS A TWIST
    WELL, THIS IS A KNIFE
    TEARS WON'T BRING HER BACK TO LIFE
    I TRIED

    WELL, THIS IS A STING
    WELL, THIS IS A BLOW
    IT WASN'T MEAN TO END LIKE THIS, YOU KNOW

    BUT THERE'S ABSOLUTELY NOTHING TO BE DONE
    SO LET'S GIVE THE PEOPLE THEIR FUN

Rinaya goes to leave her house. When she opens the door, FERN (40s) startles and embraces her.

FERN: HAVE YOU HEARD HENRY'S HAVING A BALL?
    HAVE YOU HEARD HENRY'S CHOOSING A QUEEN?
    HAVE YOU HEARD HENRY'S HAVING A BALL?
    YOU SIMPLY MUST GO, GO AND BE SEEN

Fern has a blue ball-gown, heels, jewellery and make-up in her bag. She dresses Rinaya like a mannequin.

A group of citizens wait in their finery for the ball to start.

CITIZENS:	IT'LL BE GRAND
	THE LIGHTS, THE GOWNS, THE MUSIC
	WILL BE GRAND
	THE DANCE, THE LAUGHS, LET'S DO IT
	WHEN THE MOON IS IN THE SKY
WOMEN:	I'M HOPING THAT I'LL CATCH KING HENRY'S EYE
FERN:	JUST A LITTLE MORE GLITZ
	JUST A LITTLE MORE GLOSS
	JUST A COUPLE MORE JEWELS
	AND YOU'LL LOOK A MILLION BUCKS
CITIZENS:	IT'LL BE GRAND
	THE LIGHTS, THE GOWNS, THE MUSIC
	WILL BE GRAND
	THE DANCE, THE LAUGHS, LET'S DO IT
	WHEN THE MOON IS IN THE SKY
WOMEN:	I'M HOPING THAT I'LL CATCH KING HENRY'S EYE

Henry enters the ballroom. The citizens clap. He bows and mingles with them.

Fern finishes Rinaya.

FERN: There. Now hurry to the ball. Godmother's orders.

Fern pushes her into the ballroom. Henry turns and spots Rinaya.

HENRY:	LOOK AT THE FACE THAT JUST WALKED IN THE ROOM
	SHE'S COME ON INSIDE AND REMOVED ALL THE GLOOM
	AND THE GIRL MAKES ME WANNA STEP UP AS HER GROOM
	SO LET'S START THIS
	LET'S START THIS

He approaches Rinaya.

Meanwhile, at Sera's house: Sera enters with freshly picked flowers. She chops off their ends and puts them in a vase. Penelope stares out the kitchen window.

SERA: LOOK AT THE GIRL WITH THE LONG, GOLDEN HAIR
I'VE DREAMED AND I'VE SCHEMED
THOUGHT I'D NEVER BE THERE
HER LIVING HERE, LIVING HERE
ANSWERS A PRAYER
SO LET'S START THIS
LET'S START THIS

HEN. & SERA: SOMEONE I WANT
IS RIGHT HERE BEFORE ME
SOMEONE I WANT
SO PLEASE DON'T IGNORE ME
I'LL GIVE AND I'LL GIVE
AND I'LL OFFER THE WORLD
TO SOMEONE I WANT

HENRY: SOMEONE I WANT

SERA: SOMEONE I WANT

HENRY: LOOK AT YOUR EYES
HOW THEY'RE SHINING SO BRIGHT
AND LOOK AT YOUR RING
HOW IT GLOWS IN THE NIGHT

He fondles the ring hanging from Rinaya's neck.

HENRY: AND I THINK IT'S FATE THAT WE MET HERE TONIGHT

He tugs on the ring and the string around her neck breaks. He slips the ring onto her finger.

SO LET'S START THIS
LET'S START THIS

Henry and Rinaya dance.

SERA:	LOOK HOW YOUR SMILES NEVER LAST FOR ME, PRINCESS AND I KNOW YOU THINK THAT YOUR LIFE IS A BIG MESS BUT PLEASE CAN'T YOU TRY 'COS I'M TRYING MY BEST SO LET'S START THIS OH LET'S START THIS
HEN. & SERA:	SOMEONE I WANT IS RIGHT HERE BEFORE ME SOMEONE I WANT SO PLEASE DON'T IGNORE ME I'LL GIVE AND I'LL GIVE AND I'LL OFFER THE WORLD TO SOMEONE I WANT
HENRY:	SOMEONE I WANT
SERA:	SOMEONE I WANT

Sera offers Penelope a flower.

SERA: AM I SOMEONE YOU WANT?

Penelope smiles politely and exits.

SERA: I GUESS NOT

Sera exits the other way.

RINAYA: It's almost midnight. My father will notice I'm missing.

Henry slips the ring from her finger.

HENRY: You go home. I'll take the glass ring. If we're meant to be together, I'll find you. The girl with the finger it fits.

RINAYA: I'm sure it fits plenty of fingers.

HENRY: I also know your face.

RINAYA: Under all the bruises and cinders, I'm not so sure.

Henry makes a show of pocketing the ring. He kisses her.

▪ SCENE FOURTEEN

Sera's kitchen. Penelope enters. Sera pulls out a tray of impressive-looking cupcakes.

SERA: Happy birthday.

PENELOPE: Oh. Thank you.

SERA: You didn't think I'd forget?

PENELOPE: I just don't really feel like celebrating.

Penelope spies the bowl of glossy apples on top of a shelf.

PENELOPE: I might have an apple instead.

She reaches for one. Sera swats her hand away.

SERA: Are you mad? You don't eat a witch's apples. They're poisoned. Everyone knows that.

PENELOPE: Poisoned?

SERA: Sleeping spells. You never wake up.

PENELOPE: And everyone knows that?

SERA: Yes.

PENELOPE: Well... then I'll take it outside, and pretend to have bitten it and fallen asleep. And I'm not really dead, I'm just sleeping. And then a prince will come along and kiss me! And I'll be alive again.

SERA: But your heart is missing.

PENELOPE: That could be... part of the sleeping curse.

SERA: Do you not understand that someone wants you locked up? The last time you left the cottage you were captured before the sun even moved across the sky.

Penelope spies a Golden Book under the bowl of apples. She pulls it out.

PENELOPE: It's the third book.

She flips through it.

PENELOPE: My God. Sera, I have to go back to the city. Just to look. Just to set eyes on my parents before they die, to see how my brother's doing. Please? For my birthday?

SERA: Absolutely not.

PENELOPE: I'll go in disguise.

SERA: No. I forbid you.

PENELOPE: Do you not understand I'm 18 now?

SERA: That doesn't make the slightest bit of difference.

PENELOPE: Oh, it makes all the difference.

Penelope takes the book to Sera's piano. She starts to play.

PENELOPE: DREAMS
WHERE DID THEY GO?
FLOWN WITH MY HEART
THROWN OUT THE WINDOW

EIGHTEEN
WAS SUPPOSED TO BE DIFFERENT
WAS SUPPOSED TO BE QUEEN
WITH A CROWN
WITH A CROWD
WITH A KING
WITH A WISE, GENTLE HAND
AND A GOLD DIAMOND RING
WITH THE PEOPLE WHO GLOW

AND THE PEOPLE WHO SAY
"IT'S YOUR DAY, IT'S YOUR DAY"

EIGHTEEN, EIGHTEEN
EIGHTEEN, EIGHTEEN
EIGHTEEN, EIGHTEEN,
EIGHTEEN

NOT A HOUSE IN THE WOODS
WITH THE TREES TO MY NECK
WHERE EVEN THE APPLES ARE POISONED ATTACK
AND I'M ALL ALONE
NOT A HOPE IN THE WORLD
WHEN I'M EIGHTEEN AND DEAD
AND NOT EVEN A GIRL

EIGHTEEN
EIGHTEEN
EIGHTEEN
EIGHTEEN

DREAMS
WHERE DID THEY GO?

Sera reluctantly hands Penelope the witch's hat.

- **SCENE FIFTEEN**

Some GIRLS are fixing up Rinaya's hair and accessories on her wedding day.

GIRL #1:   Aren't you excited?

RINAYA: I guess. I mean, I don't want to spend the rest of my life cleaning. I just never imagined being Henry's bride.

GIRL #2:   Then you're the only one.

GIRLS: YOU'RE ONLY FREEZING UP
             'COS THIS HAPPENED SO FAST
             WHEN YOU'RE CHOOSING A MAN
             YOU JUST CAN'T GO PAST

HE'S WEALTHY AND CHARMING
AND SO SUPER CUTE
THE ONE WE APPLAUD
AND THE ONE WE SALUTE
THERE'S NOBODY BETTER
SO GIRL JUST SURRENDER
HE'S YOUR MAN

They push Rinaya onto a public podium, where Henry is waiting.

HENRY: YOU'RE SURELY A STAR
THAT FELL FROM THE HEAVENS ABOVE
AND IT'S WONDERFUL LUCK
THAT I'M STANDING HERE IN TRUE LOVE
DO ME THE HONOUR OF TAKING MY HAND
THERE'S MAGIC INSIDE YOU I DON'T UNDERSTAND
IT'S HAPPILY EVER AFTER WHEN I AM YOUR MAN

CITIZENS: HAPPILY EVER
HAPPILY EVER
HAPPILY EVER
HE'S YOUR MAN

Rinaya slips a wedding ring on Henry's finger. Henry goes to slip one on hers, and Penelope screams.

The citizens turn and spot Penelope in witch's garb. Sera grabs Penelope's hand.

SERA: Run.

They do. The citizens give chase, leaving Rinaya and Henry alone.

RINAYA: I NEVER DID SAVE HER
I'M NOBODY'S SAVIOR
HAPPILY EVER AFTER?
YOU'RE MY MAN

Henry slips the glass ring onto her finger. They kiss.

- **SCENE SIXTEEN**

Blackness.

GEORGE: Here! Grab my hand!

Sounds of limbs on a wooden floor, a trapdoor shutting.

George lights a candle. He walks with a cane now. Penelope is curled on the floor, sobbing quietly. Sera puts an arm around her.

GEORGE: It's alright, they won't look here.

SERA: Why not?

GEORGE: I'm the hero.

Penelope looks at him, hopeful. Sera tucks Penelope's face back into Sera's shoulder.

SERA: Don't. *(to George)* That kind of hero?

GEORGE: Yes.

SERA: You look familiar.

GEORGE: So do parts of you.

Silence.

GEORGE: I told my daughter I'd watch her wedding from the window. You'd best leave when it's safe.

He limps to the next room, coughs and closes the door.

SERA: Why did you scream?

Penelope laughs.

PENELOPE: It's all wrong... My half-brother can't marry him. He certainly can't marry my half-brother. And the crowns they're getting... Did you see? They were my parents'. My parents are dead.

In the next room, George stares out the window.

GEORGE: BEFORE I MADE MY LIVING
WITH A SWORD AND WITH A SONG
I HAD AN AXE
AND JUST THE FACTS
BUT EVERYTHING WAS WRONG

Kathryn enters with Sera (4) in a red hood/cape.

WHEN YOU CAME AROUND THE BEND
WITH LITTLE RED
IT WASN'T LONG
'TIL I'D FOUGHT AWAY THE WOLVES
AND I'D WRITTEN YOU THIS SONG

He throws away his cane, younger now, and dances with Kathryn.

IT DON'T MATTER THAT THE WOLVES
ARE ON YOUR TAIL
STICK WITH ME
HER GRANNY'S HOUSE
IS NOT THE HOLY GRAIL
IT DON'T MATTER THEY REFUSE TO BUY
YOUR SCIENTIFIC REMEDIES
WHAT'S SCIENCE GOT ON FANTASY?
IMAGINATION, SEEMS TO ME
JUST A BIT OF MAGIC, SEE
THAT COULD BE OUR SECRET KEY
JUST BETWEEN US THREE
A LITTLE BIT OF MAGIC SETS YOU FREE

KATHRYN: A LITTLE BIT OF MAGIC SETS YOU FREE

BEFORE I MADE MY LIVING
WITH A MEDICINE OR TWO
AND THE MAGIC SHOW
MY HUSBAND AND I
TRAVELLED 'ROUND TO DO

BUT I KNEW
SO VERY SOON
THAT I HAD FALLEN HARD FOR YOU

>   I HAD FOUGHT AWAY MY DOUBTS
>   AND SIGNED UP FOR SOMETHING NEW
>
>   IT DON'T MATTER THAT THEY ALL
>   THINK I'M A WITCH
>   FOR EVERY CLOUD
>   THERE'S SILVER LINING
>   THIS IS OUR FIRST STITCH
>   IT DON'T MATTER THAT I'LL LIVE ACROSS
>   THE LAND A GOOD WEEK'S WALK AWAY
>   COME AND VISIT ME, WE'LL SAY
>   IT'S BRUTAL BUT YOU FOUND A WAY
>   YOUR DUTY AS A HERO, HEY
>   TO CHECK UP ON THE WITCH?
>   A LITTLE BIT OF MAGIC SETS US FREE

GEORGE: A LITTLE BIT OF MAGIC SETS US FREE

Kathryn kisses him and exits with Sera.

George coughs again. He picks up his cane, older once more.

GEORGE: AND NOW I'VE NOT SEEN YOU FOR YEARS
            I FEAR OUR MOMENT'S PASSED
            THAT YOU'RE SLEEPING IN THE HEAVENS
            AND OUR TIME HAS GONE TOO FAST

He looks towards the door, where Sera and Penelope still sit.

>   I LOOK AT HER AND SEE YOU IN HER EYES
>   AND WONDER IF IT'S TIME TO SHED
>   DISGUISES AND THE LIES
>   BUT FOREVER IS TOO SOON
>   I KNOW IT'S TRUE
>   GOODNIGHT, MY DEAREST KATHRYN...

He considers the 'I love you' at the end, but trails off: it is simply implied.

- **SCENE SEVENTEEN**

The sun rises on a new day. George is still at the window, looking frailer than ever.

RINAYA: Papa?

Rinaya enters, in a crown and fancy gown that bulges at the waist—she is six months pregnant.

RINAYA: Papa, the doctor told you to stay lying down.

GEORGE: I can't lie down for the rest of my life.

RINAYA: Papa...

GEORGE: Rina. You're a smart girl. They've seen this before. I don't have much longer, so if a sick man wants to look out the window, then he's going to look out the window.

RINAYA: Money isn't an object any more. What can I do?

GEORGE: Nothing. If they couldn't save the king and queen they can't save me.

RINAYA: I've been thinking. Did you come across a witch's cottage on your travels? To the south, in the North-North-East?

GEORGE: What of it?

RINAYA: I thought it was a fever dream, but maybe the witch can save you.

GEORGE: Witches can't even save themselves.

RINAYA: Papa—

GEORGE: You promised you'd stay.

Silence.

GEORGE: I forbid you to go to that cottage! I forbid it!

RINAYA: You forbid me?

GEORGE: Yes! You are forbidden to leave the city, but you are especially forbidden to go to that cottage!

RINAYA: I'm the queen now.

She takes his sword from the wall.

GEORGE: You put that back! Thief! I'll tell Henry!

RINAYA: Let him try and stop me.

She exits.

- **SCENE EIGHTEEN**

Rinaya travels through the forest.

RINAYA: THE PAST IS PAST
IT'S DEAD AND GONE
RIGHT NOW I'M WELL
RIGHT NOW I'M STRONG
AND THINGS ARE COMING CLEAR TO ME
THAT HERE'S WHERE I BELONG

THE PAST IS PAST
IT'S DEAD AND GONE
RIGHT NOW I'M WELL
RIGHT NOW I'M STRONG
AND THINGS ARE COMING CLEAR TO ME
THAT HERE'S WHERE I BELONG

GIVE ME THE ROAD
GIVE ME THE FOREST
GIVE ME FRESH AIR
GIVE ME ALONE
AND I WILL OWN IT

GIVE ME THE SKY
GIVE ME THE EARTH BETWEEN MY FEET

> GIVE ME A GOAL
> AND I WILL SHY FROM ALL DEFEAT

Penelope stares out Sera's tower window.

PENELOPE: THE PAST IS PAST
> IT'S DEAD AND GONE
> RIGHT NOW I'M SMALL
> RIGHT NOW I'M WRONG
> AND THINGS ARE COMING CLEAR TO ME
> IT WAS HOPELESS ALL ALONG

PEN. & RIN.: GIVE ME THE ROAD
> GIVE ME THE FOREST
> GIVE ME FRESH AIR
> GIVE ME ALONE
> AND I WILL OWN IT

Penelope spots Rinaya approaching. Penelope is ecstatic—she runs downstairs, grabs an apple, gorges a chunk out of it with her fingernails, goes outside and collapses.

RINAYA: GIVE ME THE SKY
> GIVE ME THE EARTH BETWEEN MY FEET
> GIVE ME A GOAL
> AND I WILL SHY FROM ALL DEFEAT

Rinaya kneels beside Penelope. She shakes her gently.

RINAYA: Princess? Princess?

Rinaya glances around. She kisses Penelope, who 'wakes.'

PENELOPE: I knew you'd come. You woke me—you *are* my true love!

Rinaya sits back, looks at her pregnant belly.

RINAYA: That's complicated...

Sera slams open her front door.

SERA: Stop it! Stop it now! *(points to Rinaya)* She's not a man. *(points to Penelope)* You're not cursed. *(points to

Rinaya) She's not cursed. *(points to Penelope)* She's not your true love!

TIME TO GROW UP
LITTLE GIRLS, LITTLE GIRLS
TIME TO WISE UP TO THE WAYS OF THE WORLD
THERE'S NO EASY CURE
AND THERE'S NO EASY CURSE
AND USUALLY THINGS
THEY TURN OUT FOR THE WORST

TIME TO LET GO
AT LAST, AT LAST
OF FAIRY TALE THINKING THAT'S KEEPING YOU CAST
IN ROLES OF THE DAMSEL, THE PRINCESS, THE HERO
WHEN ALL OF THOSE THINGS
HAVE AMOUNTED TO ZERO

AND YES, OF COURSE, THERE'S LIES APLENTY
THOUSANDS, THOUSANDS
FOUR AND TWENTY
BLANKETING THE WORLD
WELL, AREN'T YOU LUCKY, GIRLS?

THERE'S NO SUCH THING AS MAGIC
NO SUCH THING AS MAGIC
NO SUCH THING AS MAGIC
NEVER WAS

TIME TO FACE UP
TIME TO SEE CLEAR
WAS NEVER A SPIRIT
AND ALWAYS WAS HERE
THIS WITCH
WHICH WITCH?
AND SUCH A GLITCH
THAT I'D MAKE THIS CONFESSION
TO TEACH YOU A LESSON

I'VE LIVED MY YEARS ON LIES APLENTY
FED ON THOUSANDS
FOUR AND TWENTY

CAN'T STOMACH THEM TODAY
IT'S TIME TO PURGE AND SAY

THERE'S NO SUCH THING AS MAGIC
NO SUCH THING AS MAGIC
NO SUCH THING AS MAGIC
NEVER WAS

Sera collapses against the doorframe. Silence.

SERA: Well, say something. You gonna burn the witch? Oven's nice and hot. No one would blame you. They think I'm already dead. Playing the hero? I'll play. My world's ended anyway.

Penelope is struck dumb.

RINAYA: Can you heal my father?

- **SCENE NINETEEN**

George hobbles from the window to the bed. Sera enters, clutching a potion.

SERA: Daughter's orders.

GEORGE: I don't know you.

SERA: Your daughter does. I told her who I was.

GEORGE: Did you?

SERA: All of me.

GEORGE: Then you'd be dead.

SERA: She cares more about you than what you're supposed to do.

Rinaya enters.

SERA: *(to Rinaya)* The princess?

RINAYA: Downstairs. I had to half carry her in.

SERA: She speaks?

RINAYA: No. Seven days of silence.

GEORGE: You did save her.

RINAYA: I'll save you.

Sera offers the potion. George drinks it.

SERA: You'll need another this time tomorrow.

GEORGE: Ahhh. So we can't kill you yet.

RINAYA: Papa...

GEORGE: Stop.

RINAYA: You could have told me.

GEORGE: That I fed us on fake heroism? You would have been a liability; it was my burden to bear.

Sera looks through the window.

SERA: What is that?

Outside the window, Penelope runs across the city square. Heads turn. She runs on stage and into Henry's arms.

HENRY: Pen? Penny. Oh, God.

The citizens go wild.

SERA: *(to George)* He had the third book?

GEORGE: They both did.

Sera runs out. Rinaya follows her.

Sera reaches the stage.

SERA: You get your hands off her!

Soldiers move towards her. Sera clicks her fingers and a brief flame appears.

SERA: Stay back or the whole square goes up!

The soldiers freeze.

SERA: You took her. You took her into the forest and locked her up.

HENRY: I did no such thing.

SERA: You ordered it.

HENRY: *You* locked her up. You're not as ugly as I thought.

SERA: Spell. I took her voice and made me young. Made me pretty.

HENRY: I might not go that far.

SERA: If she wasn't in my tower she would've been in someone else's.

Penelope pulls away from Henry.

HENRY: It's okay, Penny. I never wanted anything to happen to you.

SERA: Then you shouldn't have kidnapped her!

The citizens gasp as if they haven't heard this before.

HENRY: Sometimes you have to act for the greater good. Sometimes you have to do the wrong thing for the right reasons. Sometimes you have to think about what's best for those you love. Haven't you had to do that?

SERA: Seems like that's all I've ever done.

HENRY: Penny. Love. You shouldn't have had to rule alone. You needed a prince. You needed to be captured so you could be rescued. I acted in love so you could find love. I promise. My heart broke when I thought you were dead. I was wrong. But I meant so well.

Penelope cries into his shoulder.

HENRY: Were you rescued in the end?

Penelope nods.

HENRY: Good. Good. Wonderful. Is your prince here? He can have my crown.

PENELOPE: He died. *(points to Sera)* She killed him.

The citizens react.

HENRY: That's right. They told me he never came out.

SERA: He was taking off her dress.

HENRY: So?

SERA: So he was going to take advantage of her!

HENRY: *(to Penelope)* Was he?

Penelope shakes her head.

SERA: She wouldn't know, she was asleep.

HENRY: She would've woken.

SERA: I drugged her!

HENRY: What?

SERA: For your precious greater good! For the love! So I could feed her and talk to her while you kept her locked up!

HENRY: The prince you're talking about. About my height, red hair, blue eyes? Rare combination around here. I've known him all my life, and he received an anonymous tip as to where my half-sister might be in the forest. He would never hurt her. If she wasn't waking, if she was clothed in this bloody slip, you don't think he might have looked under it for wounds? To check if she was injured?

Sera is dumbstruck.

HENRY: I don't know what you're trying to do here, but I love my sister. I wanted the best for her. You've kept her to yourself for months, you've killed what's probably her only chance for love... You kept her from her rightful place as queen....

He motions to the soldiers, who advance on Sera. Rinaya runs in front of Sera, shielding Sera's body, and throws her crown to Henry.

RINAYA: It's Penelope's.

HENRY: Rina... She is your mother only in blood, and not worth our mercy.

RINAYA: My mother?

SERA: *(sotto)* He means my mother.

RINAYA: What?

SERA: *(sotto)* She could be your mother, too. I'd believe it.

RINAYA: *(to Henry)* Well. Really? You believed this... You knew this? And you kept it from me?

HENRY: You couldn't go after her. For many reasons.

RINAYA: I can't do many things for many reasons.

Rinaya draws her sword.

HENRY: You have magic inside of you.

RINAYA: I have something inside of me.

HENRY: You have a royal child.

Silence.

RINAYA: Henry, do you love me?

HENRY: I love what you can do for the kingdom.

RINAYA: You're all as bad as each other. Something my father—the hero—taught me was honour. But I understand desperation. And I exercise compassion. And I think many people here have something in common.

A long moment. Henry places the crown on Penelope's head.

HENRY: NOT SURE I WAS RIGHT ANY MORE
WOULD I DO THE SAME AGAIN?
I'M NOT SURE
BUT I DO KNOW
I DID IT ALL FOR THE LOVE

SERA: NOT SURE IF I'D ASK FOR FORGIVENESS
I DID THE BEST I COULD
IN THIS BIG MESS
BUT I DO KNOW
I DID IT ALL FOR THE LOVE

GEORGE: WELL, I TRIED TO PROTECT
AND I TRIED TO RAISE WELL
AND IF I TAUGHT YOU SOMETHING
THEN THAT'S JUST AS WELL
AND JUST KNOW
I DID IT ALL FOR THE LOVE

ALL THREE: FOR THE LOVE

'COS EVERYONE THINKS THEY'RE DOING THE RIGHT THING
AND EVERYONE'S DOING THE BEST THEY CAN
AND I WON'T SAY I'M SORRY
'COS SOMETIMES YOU JUST HAVE TO KEEP HER SAFE
TAKE A STAND
AND SOMETIMES YOU TELL A STORY

TO MAKE THE WORLD A LITTLE BRIGHTER AGAIN
SO I SAY
I DID IT ALL FOR THE LOVE

SERA: FOR THE LOVE

HENRY: AND MAYBE IT CURDLES

SERA: AND MAYBE IT CHARS

GEORGE: AND MAYBE IT GROWS UP AND WANDERS OFF FAR

HENRY: AND MAYBE IT'S DEADLY

SERA: AND MAYBE IT'S COLD

GEORGE: AND MAYBE IT STRANGLES WHEN IT'S BIG AND OLD

HENRY: LIKE A POISON

SERA: A FLAME

GEORGE: LIKE A MONSTER LESS TAME

HENRY: LIKE A VINE

SERA: LIKE A WAVE

GEORGE: YOU CAN NO LONGER SAVE

ALL THREE: LIKE THE SUN BURNING DOWN FROM ABOVE
I DID IT, I SWEAR, FOR THE LOVE

'COS EVERYONE THINKS THEY'RE DOING THE RIGHT THING
AND EVERYONE'S DOING THE BEST THEY CAN
AND I WON'T SAY I'M SORRY
'COS SOMETIMES YOU JUST HAVE TO KEEP HER SAFE
TAKE A STAND
AND SOMETIMES YOU TELL A STORY
TO MAKE THE WORLD A LITTLE BRIGHTER AGAIN

	SO I SAY I DID IT ALL FOR THE LOVE
SERA:	FOR THE LOVE
ALL THREE:	FOR THE LOVE
SERA:	FOR THE LOVE
ALL THREE:	FOR THE LOVE
SERA:	I DID IT, I SWEAR…
ALL THREE:	FOR THE LOVE
RINAYA:	*(to Henry)* You'll look after my family?
PENELOPE:	Give her what she wants.
HENRY:	You have my word. As much as that means to you.

Silence.

RINAYA:	There's something we need to tell you about fairy tales.

END

ABOUT EPHINY GALE

Ephiny Gale was born in Melbourne, Australia, and is still there, alongside her lovely wife and a small legion of bookcases. She has written several produced stage plays and musicals, including the sold-out *How to Direct from Inside* at La Mama and *Shining Armour* at The 1812 Theatre. Her script *Time Scraps* was a finalist in St Martin's National Playwriting Competition, and *Hearts up Sleeves* won the Five Minute Play award at Dante's.

She is also the author of about a dozen short stories, novellas and novelettes, which have appeared in publications including *Daily Science Fiction*, *Aurealis* and *GigaNotoSaurus*. Her stories have featured on the Tangent Online Recommended Reading List and as a finalist in Nestlé's Write Around Australia.

When not writing, Ephiny currently works as a Project Coordinator for an online education company. Her previous roles have included coordinating a major arts festival, working as the Association Secretary for the Green Room Awards (Melbourne's premier performing arts awards), nine months as a professional wedding DJ, and working as an executive of a university student association.

Ephiny has a Masters in Arts Management, a red belt in taekwondo, and a passion for psychology, fairy tales, and storytelling in all its forms. She also especially enjoys raspberries, Italian greyhounds, playing board games with friends, and wearing clothes made out of unnatural fabrics.

More at ephinygale.com

www.ingramcontent.com/pod-product-compliance
Lightning Source LLC
Chambersburg PA
CBHW020610300426
44113CB00007B/584